READY
for
HILLARY?

READY
for
HILLARY?
PORTRAIT OF A PRESIDENT IN WAITING

ROBIN RENWICK

Biteback Publishing

First published in Great Britain in 2014 by
Biteback Publishing Ltd
Westminster Tower
3 Albert Embankment
London SE1 7SP
Copyright © Robin Renwick 2014

ISBN 978-1-84954-788-8

10 9 8 7 6 5 4 3 2 1

A CIP catalogue record for this book is available from the British Library.

Set in Stempel Garamond

Printed and bound in Great Britain by
CPI Group (UK) Ltd, Croydon CR0 4YY

CONTENTS

INTRODUCTION

URING THE BUSH/CLINTON election in
1992, I was the British ambassador in Washington. Our relationship could hardly have
been closer with the outstanding Bush foreign policy
team – Baker, Scowcroft, Colin Powell, Eagleburger,
Gates and others – but I soon discovered that the domestic policy advisors were fractious and divided and nor
was the President as interested in domestic as he was
in foreign policy, at which he excelled. It was difficult
for the government in London to believe that the victor
of the First Gulf War might be voted out of office, but
James Baker was one of those who feared that this could
happen. This caused us to take a close look at the field

of Democratic Party contenders, known at the time as the seven dwarves. The most credible of them seemed to us to be the still little-known 'New Democrat' Governor of Arkansas.

Jonathan Powell, first secretary in the embassy, was asked to follow the fledgling candidate around on the Clinton bus in New Hampshire, graduating thereafter to the Clinton campaign plane, bringing him into daily contact with many of Clinton's closest domestic policy advisors. I kept in touch with those members of the Democratic foreign policy establishment – Warren Christopher, Strobe Talbott, Tony Lake and Richard Holbrooke – who seemed most likely to feature in a Clinton administration, if there was one.

The fact that we had sought them out beforehand was appreciated by them when they descended on Washington. My friend Katharine Graham gave a dinner for the Clintons before the inauguration, at which Bill Clinton thanked me for this and I met a beaming Hillary, who invited us to dinner at the White House not long after they moved in. It was not difficult to establish a good personal relationship with Bill Clinton, as that was and is his forte – but that went for Hillary too. Far from finding her to be the left-wing virago portrayed by the right-wing talk shows, she was personally very friendly and she and her staff were unfailingly helpful.

Told that the redoubtable South African anti-apartheid campaigner Helen Suzman was staying at the embassy, Hillary turned out to know all about her, insisting on making a well-justified fuss of her at the White House. She enjoyed a lunch with Princess Diana, devoted in part to discussing how to protect their respective children from the press. Hillary was fiercely protective of Chelsea, letting the White House press corps know that they would write what they liked about her, but her daughter was off limits.

There was never any doubt at this time of the affection between the Clintons, notwithstanding the prior bimbo eruptions. Bill had only to squeeze her hand or give her a hug to produce a huge Hillary smile. They enjoyed whispering to each other, heads close together in conspiratorial fashion, a habit that has endured to this day. She also could get exasperated, as she did one evening when we were summoned together to Barbra Streisand's dressing room. Hillary was in foot-tapping 'let's get out of here' mode, while Bill fawned over the star.

As for the supposed 'project' of sixteen Clinton years, Hillary in this period, assertive and demanding within the White House, doubted if she could ever get elected anywhere 'because I am so hard-hitting'.[1] She had thought at one point of standing to succeed her husband as Governor of Arkansas, but the polls had shown that she was unelectable. She had yet to start re-inventing herself enough to open up the possibility of elective office at all. Dedicated to pursuing progressive causes, she had a tendency to believe that her opponents were not just misguided, but also wicked.

Her husband helped to turn her into an anglophile, taking her to visit his old haunts at Oxford. Visiting Europe for the fiftieth anniversary of the D-Day landings, Hillary was thrilled that they were invited to spend the night on the royal yacht, *Britannia*, becoming an admirer of the Queen and the Duke of Edinburgh, who were very welcoming to her. These days she is addicted, when she gets the chance, to *Downton Abbey*.

Though highly intelligent and extremely determined, she also was alarmingly naïve about the prospects for her great cause, healthcare reform. Having produced a fiendishly complicated draft bill over a thousand pages long, it was an absolutely traumatic shock for her to discover that there was no way she could get this passed into law and that, in the US public's opinion, the fact that she was married to the President did not entitle her to be a key domestic policy advisor.

Throughout this period, my efforts were devoted to trying to get the US to show the leadership needed to resolve the Bosnia crisis, which Europe clearly was incapable of doing. At the outset, I got no help at all from Hillary. To encourage her husband to stay out of foreign quagmires she had given him a copy of *Balkan Ghosts* by Robert Kaplan and I found Bill Clinton trying to quote to me Bismarck's statement that the whole of the Balkans was not worth the bones of a single Pomeranian grenadier. Hillary felt that people in the Balkans had been fighting each other for the past 900 years. If the US were to get involved, it would be like Vietnam.

When Katharine Graham arranged for the Clintons to meet Henry Kissinger on Martha's Vineyard, he found, to his surprise, that all they wanted to talk about was healthcare, not world affairs. When Madeleine Albright introduced them to Václav Havel, President of the Czech Republic, who wanted the US to intervene in Bosnia, it was Hillary who cut the evening short by reminding her husband that they had more pressing domestic issues to deal with.

Two years later, the situation in Bosnia had deteriorated to a point at which I was asked to tell the chairman of the US joint chiefs of staff, General Shalikashvili, that we might have to ask for US military help in extricating the British and other contingents there. Meanwhile, General Mladić and his Serb forces had massacred the male inhabitants of Srebrenica, despite the presence of the Dutch UN peacekeeping contingent there. The

British contingent in the equally vulnerable enclave of Goražde was very clearly next in line.

In these pretty dire circumstances, I asked to see the President on his own. His chief of staff, Mack McLarty, arranged this for me. I told President Clinton that if we allowed the Serbs to do in Goražde and other enclaves or in parts of Sarajevo what they had done in Srebrenica, I did not believe that the reputation of any western leader would survive, including his own. I was trying to combine my efforts with those of Richard Holbrooke and Tony Lake to get him to take decisive action.

I found to my relief that, by this stage, Bill Clinton agreed. General Rupert Smith, commanding the UN forces in Bosnia, had come to the same conclusion. A military ultimatum was delivered to General Mladić about the consequences of an attack on Goražde and the other enclaves. An attack by Serb forces on Tuzla triggered the bombing campaign that led to the Dayton Peace Accords. My White House friends had told me that I had a subterranean ally in our efforts to get the President over this line. This was Hillary, horrified by what had happened in Srebrenica and insisting that the US must respond.

Hillary today has a better chance than anyone else to be the next President of the United States. Hers has been an extraordinary political odyssey. The most damaging

strike against her, her real and perceived desire to want
to interfere in policy without being elected, was conjured away when she did get herself elected as the junior
senator for New York. This was the decisive turning
point in the story of the two Hillarys. For she found,
in running for election, that she had to listen to her
electors. When she started running for senator in that
election, her media advisor Mandy Grunwald warned
that people were used to seeing her only in 'stern' situa-
tions. In private she was chatty, humorous and friendly.
She needed to show herself to be more human and infor-
mal. Hard as she tried to take that advice to heart, in her
race against Obama, she still was held to be less likeable
than her pretty aloof opponent. Her time as Secretary
of State has helped her to develop a more mature and
less distrustful relationship with her nemesis – the press.

Hillary, contrary to belief, does have a sense of humour,
which she expresses with a surprisingly loud guffaw.
When the wife of the new head of MI6, Sir John Sawers,
posted a picture of him in a bathing suit online, he was
greeted at the UN by Hillary with the words 'Nice legs!'

There is, currently, no up-to-date study of Hillary.
This book seeks to examine, as objectively as possible,
her record to date, what it reveals about her strengths
and weaknesses, and what kind of President she would
be likely to be if she did succeed in her ambition of

becoming the first female President of the United States. In an increasingly challenging international environment, what sort of policies will she be likely to pursue towards America's friends, allies and opponents?

DEATH OF A TERRORIST

WHEN, TO HER surprise, Hillary Clinton was installed as Secretary of State by Barack Obama, the most frustrating problem with which she had to deal was that of Pakistan.

In 1995 Hillary had made a visit to Pakistan as First Lady, bonding with Benazir Bhutto, who was assassinated in 2007. By the time she returned as Secretary of State in October 2009, Benazir's husband, Asif Ali Zardari, was President. En route to Pakistan, Hillary was asked by a journalist if she was convinced that the

Pakistani military and intelligence services had cut off all ties with terrorists. No, she said, she was not.

Hillary is a passionate believer in public diplomacy, always wanting to give extended television interviews and hold 'town hall' meetings wherever she could. The surveys were showing that fewer than 10 per cent of Pakistanis had a favourable view of the United States. She faced a hostile interrogation by Pakistani TV reporters about conditions attached by Congress to the latest massive US aid allocation to Pakistan, in particular that they should contribute to the fight against the Taliban. Hillary's response was: 'Let me be very clear. You do not have to take this money. You do not have to take any aid from us.' She found Pakistanis emphasising the human and financial costs to them of a conflict they seemed to regard as having been imposed on them by the US, despite Taliban bomb explosions in Peshawar and other cities and the reign of terror they were seeking to establish in the Swat valley.

She agreed that drone attacks raised major ethical questions, in particular about civilian casualties and the need for meticulous control in authorising them. But they had also turned out to be the most effective method of dealing with senior Al Qaeda and Taliban commanders, with bin Laden himself worried about the casualties they were inflicting. She had a shouting match with her friend the CIA director Leon Panetta about whether the US ambassador in Pakistan should be informed in advance about planned drone strikes (Panetta was adamant that he should not) but, on Hillary's part, this was very much the exception, not the rule. Asked by a Pakistani student if she did not regard drone strikes as also a form of terrorism, 'No, I do not', she replied.

Having acted for three days as a punch bag (why had the US supported General Musharraf? Why did the US always support India?), Hillary responded with:

> Let me ask *you* something. Al Qaeda has had safe haven in Pakistan since 2002. I find it hard to believe that nobody in your government knows where they are and couldn't get them if they really wanted to ... So far as we know, they're in Pakistan.

This caused consternation in the Pakistan government and press. On the next day, she repeated: 'Somebody, somewhere in Pakistan, must know where these people are.'[2]

✳   ✳   ✳

In March 2011, Hillary was having lunch with Leon Panetta in her private dining room on the eighth floor of the State Department. Panetta had told her that he wanted to see her on her own. He told her that the CIA had been tracking the best lead they had had in years about the whereabouts of Osama bin Laden. She was asked to join a small group at the White House working in secret on this. The CIA believed that a 'high value' target, possibly bin Laden, was living in a walled compound in Abbottabad, not far from the Pakistani military academy. Some of the intelligence analysts were highly confident that this was bin Laden; others much less so.

They debated the options. That of sharing the intelligence with the Pakistanis was quickly dismissed: they could not be trusted. Bombing the compound, situated in a built-up area, carried with it a high risk of civilian casualties and even then it would be impossible to determine whether bin Laden had in fact been killed. A missile strike might limit the damage, but would not confirm the target. The most radical option was to insert a special forces team into a heavily populated city deep inside Pakistan. There was no doubt, as Hillary could see, that this posed by far the greatest risk, especially if the special forces ended up in a conflict with the Pakistani military, hundreds of miles from the bases from which they had flown into Pakistan.

Hillary had been the junior senator for New York on

11 September 2001. On the following morning, with US airspace closed, she flew on a special flight from Washington, then by helicopter to lower Manhattan. Smoke was still rising from the smouldering wreckage of the World Trade Center. When they landed, despite wearing a surgical mask, her lungs were filled with acrid smoke. Firemen, exhausted and covered with soot, were staggering from the wreckage. Hundreds of rescue workers had lost their lives. Over the next few days, she visited survivors, many of them with fearful burns, in the hospitals and rehabilitation centres and kept in touch with some of them, her constituents, for months afterwards. There was never any doubt what Hillary would do if she got the chance of helping to rid the world of bin Laden.

Leon Panetta recommended the special forces operation. The Defense Secretary, Bob Gates, was sceptical, recalling Carter's failed hostage rescue attempt in Iran and the 'Black Hawk down' episode in Somalia. He preferred an air strike as much less risky. The Vice-President, Joe Biden, was very doubtful. But the domestic antennae of the normally hyper-cautious Barack Obama were telling him what would happen to a President thought to have had the chance to kill bin Laden, if he failed to take it.

Admiral McRaven, commanding the Navy SEAL teams, was confident they could get the job done.

On 28 April 2011, Obama asked for their final recommendations. Hillary pointed out the potential damage to the relationship with Pakistan and the obvious risks, but came down firmly in favour of the operation. Gates had reminded them that they depended on Pakistan for the logistic support of the US forces in Afghanistan. When, in an earlier meeting, someone talked about Pakistani honour, Hillary had exploded, 'What about *our* honour?'

McRaven recommended launching the operation on the earliest moonless night, which was 30 April. Someone, apparently forgetting the time difference, objected that this was the evening of the White House correspondents' dinner, at which, once a year, the President is expected to make fun of himself (and his opponents) in front of the Washington and national press. What if he had to leave early? How would it look if the President were telling jokes while such a mission was underway? Hillary could not believe that the timing of a military mission of this importance was being discussed on such a basis. 'F*** the White House correspondents' dinner,' she declared, to the delight of Gates and the military. In the event, fog intervened on the thirtieth.

On the afternoon of 1 May, Hillary and the national security team gathered in the situation room in the White House. At 11 p.m. local time, two Black Hawk helicopters carrying Navy SEALs and three Chinook transport helicopters carrying reinforcements crossed the border into Pakistan, flying below the radar screen, but clearly visible to the team in the White House. To their alarm, the first helicopter's tail clipped the compound's wall and the second had to land outside it, instead of on the roof as planned. Hillary held her breath. The photograph of her on that day holding her hand anxiously over her mouth as they all stared at the screen 'does capture how I felt'. Obama and Gates were calm and the SEALs stormed into the compound. 'After what seemed like an eternity, but was actually fifteen minutes,' McRaven reported that the team had found bin Laden and that he was 'enemy killed in action'.[3]

Before he went on television to tell the American people what had been achieved, Obama telephoned his four surviving predecessors. When he got to Bill Clinton, he said: 'I assume Hillary's told you…' Clinton had no idea what he was talking about. Hillary had been told not to tell anyone. So she didn't tell anyone, including her husband.

CHAPTER 1

THE CLASS OF '69

ILLARY RODHAM WAS born in Chicago on 26 October 1947, a 'fortunate place and time', as she described it in her autobiography, *Living History*.⁴ With her two brothers, the family moved to the leafy middle-class suburb of Park Ridge. Her father, Hugh Rodham, whom she adored, graduated from Penn State University. He had served as a chief petty officer in the US Navy during the war, training seamen who were despatched to the Pacific theatre. An opinionated conservative Republican and a self-made small businessman, he ran his own drapery business in Chicago. He was a gruff, stern and demanding parent, descended from a line of Welsh coalminers. The children were taught self-reliance and Hillary that she needed to outperform.

Her mother, Dorothy, came from a broken and extremely impoverished home. Abandoned by her mother, she was sent by her as an eight-year-old on a four-day journey across America, in sole charge of her sister (aged three), to stay with harsh and distant grandparents, overcoming a difficult and unhappy childhood to become a classic homemaker, a way of life that was to seem un-ambitious to Hillary and her comrades at Wellesley. When asked by Hillary how she had avoided becoming embittered by her early life, she recalled the many small kindnesses shown to her by people who understood how desperately poor she was. Before meeting Hillary's father, she worked as a mother's help, then as a secretary. Hillary's parents were married shortly after Pearl Harbor. Holidays were spent in a cabin belonging to her father's family on Lake Winola in Pennsylvania.

The family were devout Methodists, as Hillary affirms she is to this day. She took and takes her religion seriously, toting a small bible around with her in the early years of her career and becoming a regular attendee at prayer breakfasts as First Lady and in the Senate.

Hillary remained close to her parents for the rest of their lives. When her father grew frail, she moved them both to be close to her in Little Rock. Her mother, who lived into her nineties, witnessed Hillary's swearing in as Secretary of State and was moved by her to Washington, first near to the Clintons and then to live with them.

Hillary, who had plenty of friends in Park Ridge, had a happy childhood. The one bane of her life as an adolescent was her extreme short-sightedness. Unwilling to wear thick glasses all the time, she had to be led around by her friend, Betsy Johnson. Her father had to drill her in maths but, otherwise, she excelled at school and started getting herself elected to various positions, beginning with captain of the safety patrol.

When in 1960 John Kennedy won the presidential election, her father was outraged. He was convinced that the narrow victory was due to electoral fraud by the Democratic Mayor of Chicago, Richard Daley. Hillary and Betsy Johnson decided to check for themselves whether registered voters really lived at the addresses they had given on Chicago's notorious South Side, horrifying her father, and finding in fact that some of them didn't.

Hillary was unconcerned about how she looked, but it was in this period that there began what she described as her 'life-long hair struggles'. She became a fan of the

Beatles and the Rolling Stones. In high school she was appointed to the 'cultural affairs committee'. She was, already at this stage, displaying most of her defining characteristics, namely her willpower, ambition and extraordinarily fierce determination.

Reminiscing about her it was clear to her classmates that she saw life as a competition, and one in which she intended to do better than the boys.

Hillary remained an active Young Republican and a self-proclaimed Goldwater girl, eagerly studying Barry Goldwater's book *The Conscience of a Conservative*. Her Methodist pastor, Don Jones, was determined to expose his students to life on the other side of the tracks in Chicago, introducing them to children from the South Side. He took them to hear a lecture by Martin Luther King, whose assertion that 'we now stand on the border of the Promised Land of integration' made a considerable impact on Hillary, the more so as Don Jones took her up on the stage to shake hands with Dr King.

In her junior year at high school, she made a speech to the student body – all 5,000 of them – with impressive self-confidence. But when she ran to be student president, she lost in the first round to her male opponents.

In November 1963, she was appalled at the assassination of John Kennedy, which led her mother to admit that she had voted for him. In the 1964 election, she threw herself unsuccessfully into campaigning as a Goldwater girl.

Graduating in 1965, as an outstanding student, she was encouraged to apply to the prestigious East Coast women's colleges of Smith and Wellesley, though to her they seemed rich, fancy and intimidating. Attending their presentations in Chicago, she was alarmed to find that the other girls seemed far more worldly than her. She chose Wellesley because of the picture of the college's lake in the brochure.

Once she got there, initially she felt very isolated. She struggled in maths and geology and her French teacher told her that her talents lay elsewhere. Boys were not allowed in the girls' rooms except from 2 p.m. to 5.30 p.m. on Sundays and there was a curfew at weekends. Her reaction to the fact that many of her classmates were better dressed and seemed better looking than her was to refuse to compete on those terms, wearing baggy outfits and thick glasses. Wellesley students, however, were taught that they were the 'cream of the cream' and that women could do anything.

Suffering at first, as she told a Chicago friend, from 'no longer being a star', she threw herself into every campus cause.

Elected president of the Young Republicans in her first year, her doubts were growing about the party's policies on civil rights and the Vietnam War. She had started reading the *New York Times*, much to her father's alarm. She stood down from her post with the Young Republicans, with her friend Betsy Griffith taking over from her.

By the time she was a junior, she had gone from being a Goldwater girl to an active supporter of the Democratic anti-war candidate, Eugene McCarthy. Martin Luther King's assassination in April 1968 filled her with personal 'grief and rage', telling a friend, 'I just can't stand this any more.' She joined a protest march in Boston, 'agonizing about the kind of future America faced'.[5] She had reached the conclusion that Wellesley was as 'unrealistic' as Park Ridge. The handful of black students at Wellesley were campaigning for more minority students and faculty members. Hillary by now was student president. Bobby Kennedy's assassination in June 1968 increased her despair about events in America.

Hillary had applied for the Wellesley summer internship programme in Washington. Despite her protests, she was allocated to a Republican group reporting to Gerald Ford and Melvin Laird. She quoted to Melvin Laird, who was to become Nixon's Secretary for Defense, Eisenhower's concerns about US involvement in land wars in Asia. She went to the Republican convention in Miami, working for Governor Nelson

Rockefeller's team in their failed attempt to wrest the nomination from Richard Nixon, confirming in her eyes the rightward drift of the Republican Party. With Betsy Johnson, she witnessed the Chicago police violently breaking up the student demonstrations against the Vietnam War outside the Democratic Party convention in Chicago.

She returned to Wellesley for her final year and was accepted to study at law school by both Harvard and Yale. Presented to a Harvard law professor as due to choose between Harvard and its close competitor, he claimed that Harvard had no close competitors and had too many women already.

It remained for her to graduate from Wellesley. Her classmate and friend Eleanor Acheson, granddaughter of Harry Truman's Secretary of State, decided that her class needed its own speaker at the graduation. 'The world was not progressing as we hoped it would. We had to sound the alarm!' The president of Wellesley reluctantly agreed. She had kept asking Hillary, as their representative, 'What do you girls want?' As Hillary confessed, 'To be fair to her, most of us had no idea.'[6]

On graduation day, 31 May 1969, she was due to speak along with the African American senator, Edward Brooke. She was having a bad hair day, made worse by her mortar board.

Hillary began by defending the 'indispensable task of criticising and constructive protest'. She talked about the gap between their expectations and what they had experienced over the past four years, causing them to question the reality of their pre-college lives and start asking questions about Wellesley's policies, civil rights, women's roles and Vietnam. She defended protest as an attempt to forge an identity and a way to come to terms with their humanness. 'We feel that our prevailing acquisitive and competitive corporate life … is not the way of life for us.' They were looking for something more 'ecstatic'. She talked of the struggle to establish mutual respect between people and their fears about the future. 'Fear is always with us, but we just don't have time for it.' She ended with a quote that 'the challenge now is to practise politics as the art of making what appears to be impossible, possible.'

This self-absorbed, pretentious, narcissistic hodge-podge was sufficiently in touch with the student zeitgeist to win her a standing ovation and some attention in the national press. She featured in *Life* magazine and gave interviews on TV in Chicago.[7] Her mother told her that opinion about her speech was divided between 'She spoke for a generation' and 'Who does she think she is?'

The president of Wellesley was not impressed. After her speech, Hillary went for a last swim in the lake, leaving her clothes and glasses in a pile on the shore. When she emerged, they had been removed by security on the instructions of the president.

The desperately earnest graduate wrote to a Chicago friend: 'I wonder who is me? I wonder if I'll ever find her. If I did, I think we'd get on famously.'[8]

In the summer she worked in Alaska, washing dishes in the McKinley National Park and sliming (de-gutting) salmon in Valdez. During a visit to Alaska when she was First Lady, she declared that sliming fish was a good preparation for life in Washington.

CHAPTER 2

FROM YALE TO LITTLE ROCK

ENTERING YALE LAW School in 1969 she was one of twenty-seven women, scarcely more than 10 per cent of the student body. In April 1970 eight leading Black Panthers were put on trial in nearby New Haven, attracting huge protests by those who believed that they had been set up by the FBI. President Nixon announced that he was sending US troops into Cambodia, sparking a fresh wave of student demonstrations. On 4 May, National Guard troops opened fire, absolutely needlessly, on students protesting at Kent

State university in Ohio. Four students were killed. Hillary took their deaths as personally as she had the assassinations of the Kennedys and Martin Luther King.

At a convention of the League of Women Voters in Washington, she denounced the invasion of Cambodia and the attacks on protesters. She had met the black American activist Marian Wright Edelman, getting a grant to work for a while at her research project in Washington, looking into the education and health of the children of migrant workers. Returning to Yale, she started to focus on how the law affected children. One of the causes she had adopted was the campaign to lower the voting age from twenty-one to eighteen, passed in 1971. One of her fellow campaigners, Vernon Jordan, asked to be introduced to 'this earnest young lady'. He and his wife Ann were to become among the Clintons' closest friends.

Hillary at this time still was making herself, in the words of one of her friends, 'deliberately unattractive'. Bill Clinton had arrived at Yale, shaggy haired and looking, in Hillary's view, more like a Viking than a Rhodes scholar returning from a two-year stint at Oxford. He was, as she put it, hard to miss. One evening in the Yale law library, as he kept looking at her, she walked over and said breezily: 'If you're going to keep looking at me, and I'm going to keep looking back, we might as well be introduced. I'm Hillary Rodham.' He was thereby spared from having to use his favourite approach tactic, which was to say: 'You're reading my favourite book!'

They started going out together in the spring of 1971. He seemed to be interested in everything she was interested in and, she found, he could talk about anything. 'I still love the way he thinks and the way he looks.'[9] He told her that, after graduation, he was determined to go home and run for office in Arkansas. She had a summer job with the left-wing law firm in Oakland, California of Treuhaft, Walker and Burnstein, working mainly on child custody cases. Bob Treuhaft and his wife, the English-born Jessica Mitford, both were former members of the Communist Party, while another partner still was one, a fact later used against Hillary by right-wing opponents, despite the fact that she appears to have been unaware of this at the time (and did not get on with Jessica Mitford).[10]

Bill Clinton had been asked to work on Senator George McGovern's presidential campaign by his campaign manager, Gary Hart, but decided to go with Hillary to California instead. On return to New Haven, they rented an apartment together, with Hillary dumping a previous boyfriend. He set up a 'McGovern for President' headquarters and passed muster on a visit to her parents, despite his Elvis side-burns. They worked together on the doomed McGovern campaign in Austin, Texas, teaming up with another long-standing friend, Betsey Wright.

On completing their law courses in the spring of 1973, Bill Clinton took her on her first visit to Europe, touring Westminster Abbey, Parliament, Stonehenge, Wales and York until, in the Lake District, Bill asked her to marry him, as he continued persistently to do, with her insisting that she needed more time.

Next he took her to Arkansas, where she met his mother, Virginia. They did not know what to make of each other, as Hillary was no Miss Arkansas, while Virginia believed in false eyelashes and bright red lipstick. Bill Clinton was teaching in the law school in Fayetteville, Arkansas, while Hillary worked for a time for the Children's Defense Fund, led by Marian Wright Edelman. A scholarly article by her, 'Children under the Law', was published in the *Harvard Educational Review* in late 1973, arguing that minors should have the same legal rights as their parents including, in exceptional circumstances, the right to take legal action against them.[11]

As Bill got ready to run for Congress, Hillary was offered a post on the staff of the Congressional judiciary committee looking to impeach President Nixon. She 'couldn't imagine a more important mission at this juncture in American history'. She worked for Bernard

Nussbaum, later to serve as the Clintons' legal counsel in the White House. They listened to all the Nixon
tapes, building up a strong case against him, only for
Nixon to resign in August 1974. She told Nussbaum
that her boyfriend was going to be President of the
United States, getting angry with him when he questioned her prediction.

In their work on the charges against Nixon, Hillary
and her colleagues were building a case that Nixon
should be impeached even though he might not actually have committed a felony. This was to be pretty much
the opposite of the case Hillary was to make against the
impeachment of her husband over the Monica Lewinsky affair.

She had been persuaded by Bill Clinton to take the
Arkansas bar exam, which she passed. She also took
the Washington DC bar exam, which, surprisingly, she
failed – a fact not revealed, even to her closest friends,
until many years later. If she had re-taken it, no doubt
she would have passed.

She told her friends that she was moving to Arkansas.
'Are you out of your mind?' they enquired. 'Why do
you want to throw away your future?' Every few miles
the friend who drove her there, Sara Ehrman, would ask
her if she knew what she was doing.

When she arrived at the University of Arkansas in

Fayetteville, Bill Clinton was preparing to try to unseat the only Republican congressman in Arkansas. She was assigned to teach criminal law and run the legal aid clinic, only to be told by one of her superiors that he did not believe in legal aid. Diane Blair, who taught political science at the university, became her closest friend. Bill Clinton had won the Democratic nomination for the Congressional seat, but lost the election by a mere 6,000 votes.

When she went on holiday, not just to Chicago, but also to New York and Washington where, clearly, she could have joined a major law firm, Bill became anxious. He bought them a house and, on her return, proposed again. They were married on 11 October 1975, with Hillary wearing a lace and muslin Victorian dress her mother had insisted at the last minute she should buy. The Arkansas press were told that she would be retaining her maiden name, Hillary Rodham, causing quite a stir. When asked many years later why she stayed with him, her reply was that no one understood her better or could make her laugh the way he did. He remained the most interesting person she had ever met.

Hillary's heart had overruled her head. She did not really want to be in Arkansas and had no intention of staying there. Nevertheless, it was quite a gamble she was taking, despite her conviction that Bill Clinton was destined for much greater things.

They were two completely different people. John Kennedy described Washington DC ironically as a combination of 'northern charm and southern efficiency'. Bill Clinton had oodles of southern charm, plus an alarming lack of discipline, which extended to organisation and time-keeping as well as to other activities. He was, arguably, even more intelligent than her, and certainly had better lateral vision, but was far less hardworking. Hillary was the polar opposite, a disciplined northern workaholic, not devoid of charm, but rarely bothering to show it. She was not gregarious at all. Hillary, however, was passionate about everything, including him.

In 1976 Bill Clinton was elected Attorney General of Arkansas. They made a two-week visit to Europe, the highlight of which for Hillary was visiting the Basque town of Guernica, the site of Picasso's masterpiece.

She and Bill had met Jimmy Carter a year before at the University of Arkansas. He had introduced himself by saying that he was going to be President. Bill Clinton was asked to run his campaign in Arkansas and Hillary to help in Indiana.

They moved to Little Rock. As Hillary could no longer teach at the university in Fayetteville, she had to get a job to supplement Bill's salary of $26,500 per annum. The Rose law firm was the best-known and oldest law firm in Arkansas. She had got to know one of the partners, Vince Foster, through her work at the legal aid clinic. The firm now offered her a job in the litigation section. She and Vince Foster had adjoining offices and shared a secretary.

In 1978 Bill Clinton was elected Governor of Arkansas. The Governor's pay was now $35,000 a year and they were living at state expense in the Governor's mansion, but Hillary was anxious to build up some kind of nest egg. Diane Blair's husband Jim was a successful commodities trader. Hillary invested $1,000 and walked away with $100,000, a very unusually high gain. There was no suggestion that she had done anything wrong, though those trading on her behalf may have done her some favours as she seems never to have been asked to put up funds for margin calls on the trades being made for her.

In 1978 the Clintons entered into a partnership with Jim and Susan McDougal to buy 230 acres of land on the banks of the White River in northern Arkansas. They hoped to sub-divide the site for vacation homes. The price was $20,261,120, the bulk of which was put up by McDougal. The property was held through the Whitewater Development Company. They were passive investors, with Jim McDougal running the business. As interest rates climbed to near 20 per cent, it became impossible to sell second homes. They wrote occasional cheques to make interest payments. They had no idea that Jim McDougal was engaging in complex and dubious business practices.

As the freshly inaugurated Governor, Bill Clinton made a lot of mistakes. He turned out not to be very good at governing, much preferring to debate the issues from every angle to taking a decision. He brought in his legislative assistants from outside the state, offending the locals. They also were offended by Hillary's 'don't care' appearance, determination to keep her maiden name, assertiveness and bluntness. While Bill Clinton would always seek to avoid saying no, this was not a trait associated with Hillary. She was determined to improve education in the state, launching a summer programme for talented high school pupils.

She had, meanwhile, maintained her close links with liberal and social reform groups in Washington. In 1979 Jimmy Carter appointed her to the board of the Legal Services Corporation, which funded legal services for the poor across the United States. Within a few months, the White House proposed her as chairman of the board. When Ronald Reagan became President, he proposed to end funding for the LSC, a move stymied by Hillary and her colleagues on the board.[12]

On 27 February 1980, Chelsea Clinton was born,

named after their favourite Joni Mitchell song, 'Chelsea Morning'. By now the Governor was up for re-election. The economy was struggling and rioting broke out in a camp for Cuban refugees that Bill Clinton had been persuaded by President Carter to accept in Arkansas. Hillary was very active in organising the campaign, giving staffers their marching orders, but she was herself a target for their opponents.

Bill Clinton was narrowly defeated. Both of them took the defeat very hard, with Hillary criticising her husband for his mistakes, while he appeared disbelieving and disoriented. When Hillary launched into a tirade, it could be very stinging. She recruited Betsey Wright to be his new campaign manager. At a post-election meeting addressed by the new Governor, Frank White, Hillary surfaced to attack him personally for the negative adverts about the Cuban refugee camp.

Chelsea, said Hillary, was the only bright spot in the months that followed. Bill took a job at a local law firm. Hillary had been warned that some Arkansas voters were seriously offended by the fact that she had kept her maiden name. Vernon Jordan came to stay and urged her to start using her husband's name. She decided that it was more important for her husband to become Governor again than for her to stick to being just Hillary Rodham. She was determined, however, to remain Hillary Rodham Clinton, as she is to this day. When confronted as First Lady with some note-paper entitled 'Hillary Clinton', it all had to be re-printed. She also lightened her hair and started wearing contact lenses and smarter clothes.

An inveterate believer in attack rather than defence, in the 1982 governorship campaign she continued attending Frank White's meetings and shouting questions at him, causing the Governor to retreat as soon as his speech was finished. When Bill Clinton won the election, a new Hillary appeared, elaborately dressed up for the inaugural celebrations.

He appointed her as chairman of the task force to help tackle education. The key reform issue was mandatory teacher testing, fiercely opposed by the teachers' union. She felt that public speaking was one of her strong suits, though she was always better at argument and knowledge of the facts than any attempt at humour.

In July 1983 she addressed a joint session of the Arkansas Senate and House legislative committee, analysing why the state had such a poor educational record and what needed to be done about it. At the end of her presentation a local rancher with the unlikely name of Lloyd George roared: 'Well, fellas, it looks like we might have elected the wrong Clinton!' By the end of their term, the bulk of the Arkansas budget was being spent

on education. Hillary, meanwhile, had been invited to
join the board of Wal-Mart, helping to guide their envi-
ronmental policy.

At the Rose law firm, she continued to work in close
partnership with Vince Foster and, to a lesser degree,
with Webster Hubbell. The Clintons' pollster and
advisor, Dick Morris, warned her that she should not
benefit from any fees earned from the state; she asserted
subsequently that she did not do so. But she did do
some work for Jim McDougal's firm, Madison, until
it hit the buffers with the regulators. Dick Morris also
urged her not to build a swimming pool at the Governor's mansion, advice she ignored, declaring that lots
of people had swimming pools. She did not get on with
the state troopers, who considered her to be haughty,
one of them later making the allegation, for which there
is no evidence, that she had an affair with Vince Foster.

By 1987 Bill Clinton, aged forty, was chairman of
the National Governors' Association and was debating whether to run in the election against George H.
W. Bush. Hillary thought that Bush would be hard
to beat, but Bernard Nussbaum was told by her not to
commit to anyone else. They agreed on a deadline of
14 July for him to decide as, in her own words, 'anyone
who knows Bill Clinton understands he has to have a
deadline or he will continue to explore every pro and

con'.[13] Hillary believed that the main reason he decided
not to run was Chelsea.

There was another reason, however. Betsey Wright
gave him a straightforward lecture about the number
of women he was reputed to have had affairs with in
Little Rock. If he did run, how was he going to explain
away each and every one of them?

As a result, Clinton held a press conference to explain
that he would not be running, as their seven-year-old
daughter was 'the most important person in the world
for us'. Despite her own reservations, Hillary appeared
crestfallen, fearing that he might have missed his chance
for good.

The Democratic Party nominee, Governor Michael
Dukakis of Massachusetts, asked the young Governor
to give the nominating speech at the Democratic convention in Atlanta. The result, as Hillary acknowledged,
was a fiasco. The speech was so interminably long that
delegates started yelling at the speaker to finish. A week
later, Bill Clinton re-invented himself, as he succeeded
periodically in doing throughout his career, by playing
the saxophone on the Johnny Carson show.

When Bill Clinton was re-elected as Governor
in 1990, some of his Democratic Party counterparts
started talking to him about running against Bush seeking re-election. Although the President's popularity was

sky high because of the First Gulf War, both Bill and Hillary believed that he was out of touch with ordinary Americans. Sitting next to him at a dinner at Monticello, Hillary told George Bush that in terms of infant mortality, the US had a worse record than eighteen other countries. He did not believe this but, on checking, it turned out to be true. Chelsea, now eleven, thought her father could be a good President. As Senator Tom Harkin of Iowa was running, Bill Clinton's plan was to skip the Iowa caucuses to compete with Senator Paul Tsongas for the moderate Democrat vote in New Hampshire.

In 1989 Bill Clinton had become chairman of the Democratic Leadership Council (DLC), a group of moderate Democrats, formed to campaign against the left to make the party more electable. Clinton's speech to the DLC conference in May 1991 attracted praise and attention as a sort of manifesto for the self-styled 'New Democrats'. He formally launched his campaign in September 1991. With the Hamlet-like Governor Mario Cuomo of New York, who would have been the firm favourite, staying on the side-lines, the Democratic field at this point was described by the press as the 'seven dwarves', none of whom had much national recognition.

Clinton had put together an impressive campaign team, including James Carville, Paul Begala, Rahm

Emmanuel, Bruce Reed and Al From, with George Stephanopoulos as press spokesman. To help her, Hillary recruited Maggie Williams, with whom she had worked at the Children's Defense Fund, Patti Solis, from a Mexican immigrant family, as her scheduler and Capricia Marshall. Brooke Shearer, wife of Bill Clinton's Oxford friend, Strobe Talbott, also offered to help.

---- CHAPTER 3 ----

'TWO FOR THE PRICE OF ONE'

CAMPAIGNING IN NEW Hampshire, Bill Clinton described the work Hillary had been doing for many years on children's issues and joked that he had a new campaign slogan: 'Buy one, get one free.' She fully intended, as she put it, to be an 'active partner' in his administration. The slogan was used against them to suggest that she had ambitions to be co-President with her husband.

Hillary then proceeded, as she admitted herself, to make two major *faux pas* in the campaign.

To deal with the allegations that Bill Clinton had a long-standing affair with a cabaret artist called Gennifer Flowers, she had to join him in an excruciating interview on 26 January 1992 on *60 Minutes*. The interviewer asked Bill Clinton whether he had committed adultery. He declined to answer the question, but admitted having caused pain in their marriage. The interviewer said that they seemed to have reached some sort of 'understanding and arrangement'. Bill Clinton protested that they loved each other. Hillary wished she had left things at that. Instead she said: 'I'm not sitting here, some little woman standing by my man like Tammy Wynette. I'm sitting here because I love him.'

The fallout was instantaneous and, as she admitted, deserved. She had to apologise personally to the singer Tammy Wynette and, later, in a television interview.

There followed an attack on her by a rival Democratic Party candidate, Jerry Brown, former Governor of California, accusing her of a conflict of interest in working for the Rose law firm while her husband was Governor of Arkansas. She told a TV reporter that 'I suppose I could have stayed home and baked cookies and had teas', but what she had decided to do was follow her profession. This went down extremely badly with a large number of stay-at-home mothers.

It was Hillary who christened their campaign office

a war room. Private polling at this time by Stan Green-
berg for the Clinton campaign showed that while Bill
Clinton was regarded as slick, Hillary was felt to be
ruthless. The right-wing *American Spectator* denounced
her as 'the Lady Macbeth of Little Rock'![14] Hillary was
well aware that to stifle further bimbo stories, the Clinton campaign team had persuaded a number of women
who might be suspected of having had a fling with the
Governor to sign statements that they hadn't.

Meanwhile, her more fashion-conscious friends had
decided that she needed a serious make-over. Her trade-
mark headbands, they told her, had to go. A Los Angeles
stylist was produced to cut her hair.

While she remained influential behind the scenes,
in public she was persuaded to say little more, as the
Clintons embarked on an extended bus tour with Bill's
running mate, Al Gore, and his wife, Tipper.

The Bush campaign lacked energy, reflecting the
weakness and divisions of his domestic policy advisors, in contrast to the excellence of the strongest foreign
policy team since the days of Acheson and Marshall.
The economy was weak in the aftermath of the war and
the Federal Reserve was slow in cutting interest rates.

The maverick independent, Ross Perot, also was a
complicating factor. George Bush himself had declared
that he did not really do the 'vision thing', a handicap

in a country that looks for that in its leaders. The reality was that George Bush was a great public servant, rather than a politician. To Baker's dismay, he could not bring himself to dump his unpopular running mate, Dan Quayle. Nor could he bring himself to launch character attacks on his opponent or to ask him in the debates what made him think he was fitted to be commander in chief, a question Clinton was dreading.

Bill Clinton ran a skilful campaign, with a more effective team, concentrating on the economy. As a newcomer, however, until recently very little known, a main factor in his victory was the very weak campaign waged by his opponent. The Clintons themselves, for all their ambition and confidence, experienced a degree of disbelief at suddenly finding themselves propelled into the White House. Bill Clinton won with just 43 per cent of the vote, against 37 per cent for George Bush and 19 per cent for Ross Perot.

*   *   *

As they moved into the White House, Hillary and her staff, led by Maggie Williams, were determined to demonstrate that she was going to be involved in working on the President's agenda to a very different degree to any other First Lady. This they did by insisting on offices, alongside the domestic policy staff, in the West Wing, nerve centre of the Presidency. Melanne Verveer became her very capable deputy chief of staff. Their domain became known as Hillaryland. Her staff prided themselves on 'discretion, loyalty and camaraderie and we had our own special ethos. While the West Wing had a tendency to leak, Hillaryland never did.'[15] They even had lapel buttons with 'Hillaryland' on them.

Having learned to be distrustful of the press, one of Hillary's first acts in the White House was to block off the corridor which, hitherto, had allowed correspondents to walk into the office of the President's press secretary. She had initially wanted to exile them all from the White House to the Old Executive Office Building.

Egged on by Hillary, Bill Clinton had decided to make healthcare reform the first great cause of his Presidency. Devising the reform plan for universal healthcare insurance was entrusted to the Clintons' business consultant friend, Ira Magaziner. With extraordinary naïveté, they hoped to get the legislation passed within a hundred days.

Hillary could not be appointed to a post in the administration because of the anti-nepotism laws passed after Robert Kennedy's appointment as Attorney General, but the White House announced that she would be chairing the task force on healthcare reform and charged with its legislative enactment.

At the time, thirty-seven million Americans were estimated to be without insurance and therefore having to pay for their own healthcare, if they were able to, except in an emergency, when hospitals and doctors did frequently provide free treatment. Mario Cuomo asked her what she had done to make her husband so mad at her as to give her this near-impossible task.

The Democrats themselves were divided about healthcare reform. No one was advocating the European state-funded model. Hillary found herself bumping into Congressional heavyweights on her own side – Dick Gephardt, Pat Moynihan and Robert Byrd – all with very different opinions. Magaziner's task force group grew until it was nominally 600 strong. Opponents challenged Hillary's legal right to chair the group, as she was not a government employee. The only hope of getting a healthcare bill passed quickly was to tack it to the budget resolution bill, which required only a simple majority and could not be filibustered. Both Bill and Hillary signed on for this hazardous strategy, only for it to be blocked by Senator Byrd.

At this point Hillary's father suffered a devastating stroke. Hillary abandoned her schedule to spend two weeks with him and her family in Little Rock. She made an emotional speech in Austin, Texas, as her father was dying, about the need to 're-mould society by re-defining what it means to be a human being' and asking 'Who will lead us out of this spiritual vacuum?' causing the *New York Times* to mock her as 'Saint Hillary'.[16]

She got very upset when the secret service clumsily searched their rooms at Camp David, leaving them in disarray, and at stories said to emanate from them about fierce rows with her husband, including throwing things at him.

The next serious misstep was over the travel office at the White House. The staff were popular with the press, whose travel they arranged for them. An audit found some irregularities, the staff were fired and a relative of Clinton's was put temporarily in charge. Two members of the White House staff, one of them Hillary's former law partner, Bill Kennedy, were censured publicly for their handling of the matter. As Hillary subsequently acknowledged, it was a disaster in terms of dealing with the White House press. The *Wall Street Journal* started attacking the Arkansas lawyers in the White House, including Vince Foster.

Hillary confessed that through this period she saw very little of her former partner, mentor and close friend. Their roles had reversed and she could be peremptory and demanding. On 20 July 1993, having just returned from a visit to Japan, the White House chief of staff,

Mack McLarty, telephoned to tell her that Vince Foster had shot himself in a park in Washington DC.

Two days after his death the White House counsel, Bernie Nussbaum, went through the papers in Vince Foster's office. He found personal files about the work Foster had done for the Clintons on the Whitewater land deal. He gave the files to Maggie Williams, who transferred them to Bob Barnett, the Clintons' private attorney. Hillary considered this to be legal and justifiable, but it gave rise to a myriad stories that Foster 'knew about Whitewater'. Poor Foster had left a torn-up note in his briefcase saying that 'I was not meant for the job in the spotlight of public life in Washington. Here ruining people is considered sport … The public will never believe the innocence of the Clintons … The WSJ editors lie without consequence.'[17]

Bill Clinton, meanwhile, had managed to get his budget plan cutting the deficit through the Senate, though only by Al Gore's casting vote. Hillary wanted to press ahead with her healthcare plan, but the Treasury Secretary, Lloyd Bentsen, Secretary of State Warren Christopher, and Clinton's chief economic advisor, Bob Rubin, were adamant that the next priority must be to get the North American Free Trade Agreement (NAFTA) through.

On 20 September Bill Clinton made his speech to

Congress outlining the healthcare plan. On 28 September Hillary delivered her own address to the House ways and means committee – an entirely new departure for any First Lady. The speech and her other performances before Congressional committees were warmly received, leading her to believe that there was more support for her 1,342-page, immensely complicated plan than in fact existed. What the hard-bitten senators and congressmen were applauding was the performance, not the content. Bentsen, Rubin and other members of the Clinton economic team were alarmed at the complete inability of the task force to provide any convincing cost estimates for the scheme they were working on, while suggesting that it would, somehow, pay for itself. In the view of tough-minded Southern senators like Richard Shelby and John Breaux, this was the approach of 'snake oil salesmen'.

In November 1993 Whitewater came back to haunt them when Jim McDougal was investigated for diverting funds from the Madison Guaranty savings and loan business, which he also controlled. This led to what Hillary regarded as an apparently endless 'investigation as a weapon for political destruction'. While Hillary by now had made plenty of political mistakes, and it was the height of folly for Nussbaum to have removed the documents from Vince Foster's office, successive investigations into Whitewater never succeeded in demonstrating anything more than that the Clintons had made a bad investment, with a dubious business partner, with whom they had subsequently fallen out.

Within the White House, Hillary was very controlling. She was adamantly opposed to releasing the Whitewater documents or her billing records for the Rose law firm, all of which were bound to come out in the end anyway. The press frenzy about Whitewater became so intense that the White House media team, led by George Stephanopoulos, advised the President that the only way for him to draw a line under the story was to appoint a special prosecutor, which he was not obliged to do. Some Democratic legislators, including Senator Patrick Moynihan, influenced by the fact that the campaign was being led by the *New York Times* and *Washington Post*, also were calling publicly for this. Hillary and the White House legal counsel, Bernie Nussbaum, argued fiercely against it on the grounds that this would turn into an open-ended, never-ending inquiry. They were overruled by Bill Clinton, though their predictions turned out to be accurate. The Attorney General, Janet Reno, announced the appointment of a respected judge (and moderate Republican), Robert Fiske, as special prosecutor.

In his state of the union address in January 1994 Bill

Clinton, egged on by Hillary and against the advice of senior White House staff, vowed to veto any new healthcare bill that did not provide for universal coverage, thereby limiting the scope for any compromise. Roger Altman, the outstandingly able deputy Secretary to the Treasury, resigned over his contacts with the White House over Whitewater. With greater reason, Bernie Nussbaum also resigned. In March, another former partner of the Rose law firm and friend of Hillary, Webster Hubbell, resigned from the Justice Department following accusations by his former partners about questionable billing practices. Of the team the Clintons had brought with them from Arkansas, the admirable Mack McLarty was pretty well the only one left standing.

All this had taken a toll on Hillary's relations with the White House press corps, who, from the outset, she had sought to keep at a distance.

Meanwhile she felt that they were losing the public relations war on healthcare reform. The pharmaceutical industry disliked controls on the prices of prescription drugs and the healthcare insurance industry preferred things the way they were. There was a general dislike of European 'socialised medicine' as, supposedly, of poor quality and alien to America. Hillary felt that they were on the front lines of an increasingly deep ideological divide between the Democrats and a Republican Party swinging steadily further to the right. The right-wing columnist Bill Kristol was advocating no compromise: the Republicans must simply kill the healthcare bill.

Hillary had expected Democratic senators and congressmen to fall in line behind the White House. She felt that the new President, who had won with a minority of votes in a three-way election, had far more of a mandate for change than was in fact the case. She seriously offended two very important Democratic senators who had doubts about her scheme, Bill Bradley and Patrick Moynihan, by threatening to 'demonise' those who failed to support it, leading them to conclude that she was self-righteous and arrogant.[18] A senior member of the White House staff at this time observed to me that she had a 'tin ear' politically.

＊   ＊   ＊

Hillary accompanied Al and Tipper Gore to South Africa for the inauguration of Nelson Mandela as the country's first democratically elected President. Fidel Castro was also present and at the reception afterwards Hillary was instructed not to let him meet her. Whenever she saw him moving towards her 'I'd hightail it to a far corner of the room. It was ridiculous,' she observed.[19]

Showing a complete misunderstanding of the nature of Hillary, the press seemed surprised that she enjoyed herself dancing during the celebrations.

In June 1994 the Clintons travelled to England for the fiftieth anniversary of the invasion of Normandy. They were invited to spend the night on the royal yacht, *Britannia*. Hillary professed admiration for the Queen and enjoyed meeting Prince Charles and, especially, Princess Diana, whom she admired for her campaigns about AIDS and land-mines and as a mother concerned, like her, to shelter her children as much as she could from the press.

Her husband's relations with the military, she acknowledged, had got off to a rocky start. Apart from his avoidance of service in Vietnam – avoided also by George W. Bush – he had faced immediate difficulties with General Colin Powell and the chiefs of staff over his stance on gays in the military, eventually agreeing to the 'Don't Ask, Don't Tell' compromise, with Hillary feeling that this did not go far enough.

The special prosecutor, Robert Fiske, meanwhile, had issued an interim report concluding that Vince Foster's death had been a suicide and not related to Whitewater. He was replaced by a new and far more hostile independent counsel, Kenneth Starr, a prominent Republican, who had served as Solicitor General in the

Bush administration and who Hillary regarded as bent on pursuing a vendetta against them. The investigation led by Starr was to last five years, with the Clintons convinced that the objective was to destroy them politically.

Hillary started very belatedly to try to work with the moderate Republican senator John Chafee, himself an advocate of healthcare reform, to try to find a compromise, but the positions by now were too entrenched. Hillary wanted to force the bill to a vote, to go down fighting, even if they were bound to lose. A more cautious view prevailed. After twenty months, the White House conceded defeat. She acknowledged that they had alienated a lot of healthcare industry experts and some Democratic legislators. The majority of Americans were not yet convinced that 'socialised medicine' would benefit them and make healthcare more affordable in the future.

Given how passionately she felt about the need for universal health insurance, the high hopes with which she had set out on her campaign and the intensity with which she had battled to keep the bill alive, this was for Hillary a devastating political blow, re-defining her role as First Lady.

CHAPTER 4

RE-INVENTING HILLARY

THE 1994 MID-TERM Congressional elections were a disaster for the Democrats, who lost control of both Houses of Congress. Hillary had been cheered up by a visit the Clintons made to the Middle East, where her forty-seventh birthday was celebrated by her hosts in Egypt, Israel and Jordan. She was impressed by the Mubaraks, noting the dilemma he faced in governing a country beset by tensions between a western-oriented, educated minority that wanted to pursue modernisation, and the more conservative majority, plus criticisms that he was too autocratic. She admired King Hussein and Prime Minister Rabin, and their wives, for their commitment to try to improve the situation in their region.

Hillary continued to regard Eleanor Roosevelt as a role model for her, given that she had campaigned for civil rights, child labour laws, refugees and human rights. She too had been criticised by the press for seeking to re-define the role of First Lady and failing to 'stick to her knitting'. To the amusement of the press, Hillary was reported as having imaginary conversations with her predecessor.

The despondent Hillary had an emotional meeting with her senior staffers and closest female friends. She felt like giving up, she said. She couldn't give up, they told her. She was a role model for all of them. She had, however, suffered a serious loss of influence within the White House, as Bill Clinton veered sharply back to the centre and was markedly less deferential about her advice.

Hillary herself became more disengaged, no longer attending White House strategy meetings. As some Republicans had suggested that the children of welfare mothers could be placed in orphanages, however, she picked a winning fight with the bombastic Speaker of the House of Representatives, Newt Gingrich, about this. The exchange encouraged her to take refuge in writing a book about bringing up children. The title was based on an African saying that 'it takes a village to raise a child', with the text extolling community efforts to support parents in raising children. For the next several months Hillary immersed herself in this project, with the help of a talented editor at Simon & Schuster and a Georgetown University professor of journalism, Barbara Feinman. Hillary, who had worked hard on the book, was so sensitive about suggestions that it might have been ghost-written for her that she failed to acknowledge Feinman's contribution.

In March 1995 she made her first extended trip abroad without her husband, but accompanied by Chelsea. Her first stop was in Islamabad in Pakistan, where she got on well with Benazir Bhutto, while noting that her husband was strongly suspected of corruption. They flew on to India, Nepal, where they rode on an elephant, and Bangladesh. Everywhere Hillary showed an interest in her favourite issues and found, for the first time in her life, that she had a more relaxed relationship with the accompanying press.

In May 1995, however, the new Republican-controlled Senate set up a committee led by Senator Alfonse D'Amato to investigate Whitewater. Betsey Wright and Hillary's chief of staff, Maggie Williams, were summoned to appear before it. Williams was left in tears by questions about her role in the removal of papers from Vince Foster's office.

With the press continuing to harass her about White-water and the Rose law firm, Hillary's press secretary, Lisa Caputo, was reduced to suggesting that she should give more regional interviews to 'help us get around her aversion to the Washington media' and the tone of the national press.[20]

In September 1995, Hillary attended the UN conference on women in Beijing. Given the Chinese attitude to dissidents, there was some opposition to her attending. She wanted to 'push the envelope' in her speech. She was dismayed to find that her Chinese hosts had banished the women activists attending the meeting to a camp at Huairou, an hour outside the capital, and had barred women from Tibet and Taiwan from attending it. In her speech she went through the myriad ways in which women were discriminated against and victimised, declaring that 'human rights are women's rights and women's rights are human rights, once and for all'. She added: 'Freedom means the right of people to assemble, organise and debate openly. It means respecting the views of those who may not agree with their governments. It means ... not jailing them, mistreating them or denying them their freedom or dignity because of the expression of their ideas or opinions.'

The speech earned her a standing ovation. The *New York Times* felt that it 'may have been her finest moment in public life'.[21] The Chinese government blocked any broadcasting of what she had said, but Hillary was thrilled to hear, years later, that one of her friends, visiting a bookshop in Beijing, had found them playing a recording of 'Women's rights are human rights, once and for all!'

In the same month, she entertained Queen Noor of Jordan, Leah Rabin, Suzanne Mubarak and Suha Arafat for the signing of the agreement ending Israel's occupation of some West Bank cities. She visited Latin America to meet her counterparts there, and then had to accompany her husband to Israel for the funeral of Yitzhak Rabin, killed by a right-wing extremist.

On 13 November, in the absence of any budget agreement with Gingrich and the Republicans, Clinton had to close down the government. Only 'essential' staff remained at their post. The shutdown only lasted six days, doing the Republicans more harm than the administration.

According to Hillary, Bill Clinton's relations with John Major got off to a rocky start when they learned that Major's government had cooperated with the Bush administration by attempting to unearth records of Clinton's activities in England during the student protests against the Vietnam War. Although this story was both believed and disseminated by one of their staffers, no such search ever took place, as I told Bill Clinton (but not Hillary). Relations were further strained when Clinton granted a US visa to Gerry Adams, a gamble he believed had paid off when the IRA ended up declaring a ceasefire.

Of all their trips during Clinton's Presidency, their visit to Northern Ireland in November 1995 was among the most memorable for her. There, Hillary met leaders of the women's movement for peace. They went on to Derry, home of John Hume, then back to the City Hall in Belfast and Queen's University, getting an enthusiastic welcome everywhere. In Dublin, she met the President, Mary Robinson, and Bill addressed another huge crowd.

On 3 January 1996 the White House had to hand over to the independent counsel a memo by a staffer, David Watkins, stating that it was Hillary who had insisted on firing the White House travel staff. On the following morning the Clintons' personal assistant, Carolyn Huber, suddenly discovered a new batch of Whitewater papers. There was general press incredulity as to how these had suddenly turned up.

In a *New York Times* column, William Safire called Hillary a 'congenital liar'. A *Wall Street Journal* editorial on 4 January denounced what it deemed to be a pattern of evasion of the part of the First Lady. A television interview with Barbara Walters, intended to promote *It Takes a Village*, started with the question: 'Mrs Clinton, instead of your new book being the issue, you have become the issue. How did you get into this mess, where your whole credibility is being questioned?' Barbara Walters did not understand how the documents had been so hard to find. Hillary said that there were boxes of papers all over the White House.

It was only now that her billing records at the Rose law firm were fully disclosed, revealing that she had done more work on the Madison/McDougal account than she previously had admitted. Hillary compounded the problem by claiming on National Public Radio that the Clintons had handed over all the Whitewater documents to the *New York Times* in 1992, which was what she had resisted doing. In fact, only a carefully chosen batch of documents was handed over to the *Times*, as the White House was forced to make clear.

She was now summoned by Kenneth Starr, who she considered to be hopelessly biased, to testify before a grand jury. She made the mistake of turning up for the hearing in a black cloak with a sequined dragon on the back, giving the press a field day at the expense of the 'dragon lady'. Starr's enquiry went on and on, leading to the imprisonment of Jim McDougal's wife,

Susan, for, the Clintons were convinced, refusing to incriminate them. Hillary took refuge in a tour to promote her book.

Believing, however, that she had done nothing really wrong over Whitewater or in her work at the Rose law firm, she was by now convinced that there really was a right-wing conspiracy to destroy her politically. Nor was her ire directed only at her political opponents. Stephanopoulos and others had to talk her out of declaring war on the *Washington Post*.

Encouraged in her conspiracy theories by her friend Sidney Blumenthal, Hillary was not entirely mistaken about them. The author of the main demolition jobs on her, David Brock, was subsequently to confess that he had been paid to write them by a right-wing Republican and that he regretted doing so.

Her travels abroad were doing something to rehabilitate her. She was asked to travel to Bosnia following the Dayton Accords ending the war there. Chelsea went too, as did the singer Sheryl Crow. They met local children on the tarmac, despite worries about their security, and then went on to visit the US military in Tuzla.

Next came a visit by her in July 1996, with Madeleine Albright, herself originally from the Czech Republic, to Prague to meet President Havel.

Having vetoed two welfare reform bills from the

Republicans, Bill Clinton, with Hillary's acquiescence, signed a reform bill supported by most Democrats, but which cut off benefits to immigrants, infuriating her former mentor, Marian Wright Edelman.

In August Hillary addressed the Democratic Party convention in Chicago, the only First Lady to have done so since Eleanor Roosevelt, to thunderous applause from the delegates. But, otherwise, she played little part in the 1996 presidential election, in which Clinton easily defeated the Republican candidate, Bob Dole.

There followed a visit to South Africa with Chelsea, during which Nelson Mandela showed them around Robben Island. She was now fully engaged in world tourism, writing enthusiastically about the countries she visited and people she met, though with no surprising observations about any of them.

At the G7 summit in Denver in June 1997, she had formed a friendship with Cherie Blair. Having installed Chelsea at Stanford, in late 1997 the Clintons visited the Blairs at Chequers. 'You and the Blairs are political soul mates,' she was told by her friend Sidney Blumenthal. 'New Labour' and Clinton's New Democrats had much in common. Hillary, nevertheless, was alarmed to see on television speakers at the Labour Party conference referring to each other as 'comrades'![22] They invited a group of British and American public policy figures to join the meeting, including Tony Giddens, author of *The Third Way.*

CHAPTER 5

'A VAST RIGHT-WING CONSPIRACY'

EARLY ON THE morning of 21 January 1998, Bill Clinton woke Hillary to tell her that 'there's something in today's papers that you should know about'. He told her about reports that he had had an affair with a White House intern called Monica Lewinsky and had asked her to lie about it. There had, he insisted, been no improper behaviour, but he had talked to her about job-hunting and his attention might have been misinterpreted.

Hillary wrote later that 'I will never understand what was going through my husband's mind on that day'.[23] To her, this seemed like just another political intrigue. The White House staff were in a state of shock and she knew that their attitude would be affected by hers. She recalled Eleanor Roosevelt's statement that every woman in political life must develop skin as tough as a rhinoceros hide. Asked after a speech she gave that day whether she believed the accusations were false, she said that of course she did. On 26 January, with Hillary standing beside him, Bill Clinton heatedly denied any sexual relations with Lewinsky. Hillary felt that his show of anger was justified.

On the *Today* programme, she attributed these sorts of stories to 'this vast right-wing conspiracy that has been conspiring against my husband since the day he announced for President'. A few journalists understood this, she said, 'but it has not yet been fully revealed to the American people'. At the state of the union address that evening, she was greeted with sympathetic applause. She went off to Davos to make a speech with, she acknowledged, the less than scintillating title of 'Individual and Collective Priorities for the 21st Century'.

On 5 February, they gave their largest ever White House dinner, pulling out all the stops for Tony and Cherie Blair, given their personal friendship 'as well as the historic ties and special relationship between our nations'.[24] Elton John and Stevie Wonder were asked to perform at the dinner. According to Hillary, the Speaker, Newt Gingrich, whose own infidelities were exposed later, told her that the accusations against the President were going nowhere, but subsequently led the charge for his impeachment.

They set off together on a visit to Africa, then back to China. The year before, Hillary had asked the President, Jiang Zemin, at a White House dinner for him in Washington, to explain China's repression of the Tibetans and their religion. Jiang Zemin's response was that Tibet had always been part of China; the Chinese had liberated the Tibetans from feudalism.

On the morning of 15 August, she was again woken up early by her husband to be told that the Lewinsky affair was much more serious than he had admitted. He would have to testify that there had been an inappropriate intimacy. Gulping for air, she started crying and shouting at him. He said that he had been trying to protect her and Chelsea; she was dumbfounded and outraged that she had believed him. He had lied to Chelsea too. She did not know if their marriage could survive.

Clinton made a statement half-heartedly expressing regret, to which Hillary declined to contribute: 'You're the one who got yourself into this mess.' The White

House staff, who had supported the President's denials, were demoralised and appalled.

Yet the public reactions seemed to show that most Americans regarded an affair between adults as not preventing the President from doing his job. The economy was booming and the country was at peace. His standing in the polls remained much higher than in his first term. His standing with Hillary, however, had hit rock bottom.

Within a few hours of his statement, Clinton approved a missile strike against an Osama bin Laden training camp in Afghanistan in response to the bombing by Al Qaeda of the US embassies in Kenya and Tanzania on 7 August which had killed 264 people, including twelve Americans. His opponents regarded the episode as straight out of the Dustin Hoffman film *Wag the Dog*, which portrayed a President involved with a young beret-wearing woman seeking to distract attention by bombing Albania.

Hillary's press secretary made a statement that 'clearly this is not the best day in Mrs Clinton's life. This is a time when she relies on her strong religious faith.' She described herself as feeling angry, betrayed, lonely, exasperated and humiliated.

Nevertheless, they set off for Martha's Vineyard together, with her husband banished to the downstairs bedroom. By the end of August, there was a degree of what Hillary described as détente. 'As a wife, I wanted to wring Bill's neck.' But she supported him as President. She could see no grounds to impeach him. If impeachment succeeded, she 'feared for my country'. She convinced herself that she had a higher duty. 'I knew that what I did and said in the next days and weeks would influence not just Bill's future and mine, but also America's.' She was by now in full battle mode against his and her political enemies.

In September the Clintons visited Northern Ireland with the Blairs to show support for the peace process, despite a major bomb attack by dissident republicans in Omagh. She addressed a conference of women devoted to the peace movement. Both the Clintons enjoyed the welcome they got on both sides of the border.

They returned to the White House for marital counselling sessions, but she had decided that her husband was a good person and a great President whose enemies were engaged in a political war in which she was on his side. She told her friend Diane Blair that she regarded Monica Lewinsky as a 'narcissistic loony tune' and as having thrown herself at her husband, though that did not excuse his behaviour.

She developed legalistic arguments against her husband's impeachment for 'crimes and misdemeanours', in effect ruling out lying repeatedly to the American people as a serious misdemeanour. Her personal travails were now buried a long way under her crusade to help ensure the survival of her husband's Presidency. 'By now, I wanted to save our marriage, if we could.'[25] Sixty per cent of Americans felt that Clinton should not resign, while her own approval ratings soared to nearly 70 per cent as, despite the humiliation, she stood by her man.

The glitterati rallied round her. Stevie Wonder turned up at the White House to play a song about forgiveness entitled 'You Don't Have to Walk on Water'. Anna Wintour proposed an article and photo shoot for *Vogue*. It was, she claimed, counter-intuitive for her to accept, but it did wonders for her morale (photos by Annie Leibovitz, dress by Oscar de la Renta).

Visiting the White House, Nelson Mandela said that 'our morality does not allow us to desert our friends'; the Dalai Lama told her that he was thinking of her. She told newly elected Democratic congressmen that they could not let the Republicans hound the President from office: their job was to protect the constitution.

She threw herself into a campaign to speak on behalf of Democrats under threat of losing their seats in the mid-term elections. She proved herself a terrific campaigner, more in demand than the Vice-President, Al Gore. But she developed a blood clot behind her knee

from her constant flying around the country, campaigning in twenty states, requiring her to take blood
thinners. In the elections, the Democrats fared better
than expected, making some small gains. Three days
after the election, the long-serving senator Patrick
Moynihan announced that he would not be standing
for a further term as the senior senator for New York.
She immediately was approached to consider running
as his successor.

Hillary was working hard on her appearance, spending time in the gym and adopting a new short hairstyle.
She was by this time borrowing Oscar de la Renta and
Bill Blass creations to wear at White House dinners.
Having established this network of smart and influential
friends and admirers, she had been thinking of moving
to New York when she left the White House anyway,
but worried whether their legal debts would enable
them to afford this. Moynihan's impending exit created
the opportunity for her to establish her own political
career – if she had the guts to run against the formidable Republican Mayor of New York, Rudy Giuliani.

On 16 December, with impeachment pending,
Clinton ordered missile strikes on Saddam Hussein's
military facilities in Iraq. She told Democratic members of Congress that they might be mad at Bill Clinton,
but impeachment was not the answer. When the House

of Representatives voted for impeachment, she linked arms with her husband in the Rose Garden in a show of defiance.

CHAPTER 6

'DARE TO COMPETE'

THE TRIAL IN the Senate began on 7 January 1999. A two-thirds majority, which clearly was unobtainable, was required to oblige the President to resign. She claimed that she still had no interest in running for Senator Moynihan's seat, but the Democratic leadership were determined to change her mind. Giuliani would be a tough opponent, having done much to transform the fortunes of the city during his term in office. Most of her friends and staff were against her running.

On the day, 12 February, when the Senate were voting on the impeachment of her husband, Hillary conferred for hours with Harold Ickes, Clinton's former deputy chief of staff, who persuaded her that she had to take this opportunity seriously. He described how hard she would have to work to get to know every nook and cranny of upstate New York and refute the charge of being a carpetbagger. The threat of hard work was never a deterrent for Hillary. She saw the possibility of elective office as the best answer to her critics – provided she won. If she lost, it would be liable to bring down the curtain on her political career.

The Senate, meanwhile, on 12 February, had put an end to the impeachment saga by voting on party lines against it. Helped by the sympathy vote, her positive poll ratings remained in the high sixties.

Visiting the de la Rentas at their home in the Dominican Republic, she spent her time canvassing the Dominican vote, as hundreds of thousands of Dominicans lived in New York City.

By mid-February she was indicating that she would decide about running for the Senate later in the year. Her friend and media expert Mandy Grunwald warned her not to expect a free ride from the New York press. In March she attended the 'Dare to Compete' event for young athletes in New York, only to be told by one of them: 'Dare to compete, Mrs Clinton.'[26] Two of her closest associates, Patti Solis Doyle and Maggie Williams, still were advising her not to run.

In the spring, Hillary and Chelsea visited Egypt, Morocco and Tunisia. Bill Clinton, meanwhile, was struggling with the crisis in Kosovo. The Defense Secretary, Bill Cohen, and the chairman of the joint chiefs of staff both were against the idea of bombing the Serb aggressors, pressed for by Tony Blair. Hillary was urging her husband to bomb. They must, she felt, do better in Kosovo than they had in Bosnia (somewhat ironically as she had, initially, been against any involvement in Bosnia). Clinton authorised a bombing campaign which began on 25 March. Hillary declared in Morocco that they could not permit Serb attacks on the Albanian population to continue. It took eleven weeks for the bombing campaign to succeed, but in the end the Serbs and Milošević accepted NATO demands to withdraw from Kosovo.

In New York, Hillary showed how far she still was from understanding electoral politics by really annoying a group of her supporters who had organised an event at the ritzy Le Cirque restaurant in Manhattan. Matilda Cuomo, wife of the New York Governor, had arranged a book party for *It Takes a Village*. Hillary arrived an hour late, delivered a short speech and left immediately, with no schmoozing of the socialites attending. Distinguished members of the New York media were asked to stand behind a rope in the restaurant. The event got the reactions it deserved.

Hillary was not deterred by the fact that she would be running against Giuliani, despite being denounced by him as a carpetbagger. In June she formed an exploratory committee, working with Mandy Grunwald and Bill Clinton's pollster, Mark Penn. She realised that this role reversal would be awkward for her husband. Senator Moynihan had his own reservations about Hillary, but understood the strength of support she had won in the Democratic Party in New York. On 7 July she announced her candidature at the senator's farm in New York state. She acknowledged the legitimacy of questions about her running for a state in which she had never lived but she regarded running for public office as – if she won – a form of redemption. As she strove to influence policy in the White House, she constantly had to answer the question: 'Who elected her?'

She travelled indefatigably around the rural constituencies in upstate New York. She made a bad mistake by putting on a Yankees baseball cap given to her by their manager, Joe Torre. New Yorkers considered this phoney behaviour for a girl from Chicago. Worse was to come when she made a visit to Israel and embraced

Yasser Arafat's wife, Suha, only to discover that in her speech, in Arabic, Suha Arafat had accused Israel of using poison gas to control the Palestinians.

The Clintons bought a colonial-style house in Chappaqua, an hour north of New York City. Their favourite fund-raiser, Terry McAuliffe, was raising the money to pay off their legal debts and Simon & Schuster gave her an $8 million advance for her memoir, *Living History*. Chelsea was turning out to be an asset on the campaign trail. Giuliani was not as yet making much of an effort outside New York. He also had hardly any support among the minorities and created a storm by releasing the criminal record of a black New Yorker shot dead by the police. After months trailing him, Hillary by now was ahead in the polls.

On 19 May, Rudy Giuliani suddenly announced that he was withdrawing from the race because of prostate cancer. He also was having to contend with reports of an extramarital affair. Yet his withdrawal was completely unexpected. If he had remained in the race, he would have been a far more formidable opponent than the new Republican nominee, congressman Rick Lazio.

Hillary took time out from the campaign to visit her closest friend, Diane Blair, who was dying from lung cancer. She followed the two-week effort Bill Clinton made at Camp David to persuade the Israeli Prime

Minister, Ehud Barak, and Yasser Arafat to reach a peace accord. Barak, she concluded, was willing to make peace and Arafat was not.

In August, both Clintons addressed the Democratic Party convention in Los Angeles, which nominated Al Gore to run against George W. Bush. In a television debate with Lazio, she faced a grilling from the moderator, Tim Russert, about her husband lying to her and the country about Monica Lewinsky and her reference to a 'vast right-wing conspiracy'. She coped by saying that it was a very painful time in her life.

Lazio made a mistake by saying that the upstate economy had 'turned the corner', which was not how it looked to those living there. He also marched across the stage demanding that she should sign forthwith a document agreeing not to raise so-called soft money, funds spent by outside political committees on a candidate or an issue. While this left her flustered, he was felt by the media to have 'invaded her space'. The two traded allegations, including an attack by her on Lazio for failing to support funding for breast cancer research. She won the election easily, by 55 to 43 per cent.

She was dismayed by the result of the national election, with Al Gore winning 500,000 more votes, but losing to George W. Bush. She regarded the 5:4 decision of the Supreme Court to stop a re-count in Florida as a 'blatant abuse of judicial power'. Her husband, though still the President, had to witness her swearing into the Senate from the visitors' gallery.

CHAPTER 7

AMBUSH IN IOWA

B Y THE TIME George W. Bush was ready to stand for re-election in 2004, Hillary had entrenched her position as one of the most popular Democratic politicians in the country. She still was the *bête noire* of the Republican right, for reasons she could never fully understand, but she had more popular support than the Democratic contenders lining up to challenge George Bush. There were a host of people telling her that she would be a far stronger candidate than the eventual Democratic nominee, John Kerry, or any of his challengers – John Edwards, Dick Gephardt or Howard Dean. The polls had her within striking distance of Bush and way ahead of any other Democratic candidate.

Within her entourage, two of her very closest associates, Maggie Williams and Patti Solis Doyle, believed that she could unseat the President, embroiled in a Middle East war. Nevertheless, in August she told the press that she was 'absolutely ruling this out'. She had promised to serve a full six years as the senator for New York and feared denunciation as a carpetbagging opportunist if she failed to honour that pledge.

Yet she told James Carville, who had played a leading role in the Clinton presidential campaign in 1992 (but who also had advised her against running for the Senate), that she was convinced that Bush could be beaten, but not by anyone in the current field. Before the filing deadline for the main primary elections in December, she had a meeting with the inner circle of her advisors – her husband, Chelsea, Williams and Patti Solis Doyle among them. Bill Clinton favoured her running and believed that she could win. Chelsea was against, on the grounds that she was pledged to finish her term in the Senate and would face a violent reaction if she failed to do so.

Hillary's decision was not to run. The Senate pledge

no doubt was a serious factor, though others, including her husband, had broken such pledges with impunity. She did not under-estimate George W. Bush's political skills. He was far more effective in domestic politics than his father, but on the Republican side, he had no obvious successor. All in all, 2008 looked a better bet to her than 2004.

At the Democratic Party convention in Boston in August 2005, the party faithful were enthralled by a mesmerising speech by the new Democratic candidate for the Senate from Chicago, Barack Obama. His theme was a call for unity, rejecting the sharp divide between Democrats and Republicans and the politics of cynicism, in favour of 'the politics of hope'. Both the Clintons, who had helped with fund-raising events for him and praised his potential to the skies, saw him as a favour-ite protégé.

In 2006 Hillary was seen, in Democratic Party terms, as the heir apparent and by miles the frontrunner in the next contest for the White House. She had worked hard to earn the respect of her fellow senators, includ-ing Republicans. The polls showed her popular appeal, but also some persistently high negative ratings. She remained a favourite target of the right-wing talk shows.

Her vote in 2002 in favour of the Iraq war, which she had cast at least in part to burnish her foreign and defence policy credentials vis-à-vis her expected Republican opponents, had become increasingly toxic with the left wing of the Democratic Party as the war dragged on with no victory in sight and became increasingly unpopular.

The other worry among some of her colleagues still was about her husband. Rumours continued to circulate about his private life. Well founded or not, they were believed by many and eagerly disseminated by his foes. The other concern was that he might be too dominant an influence on Hillary and in her administration, if she got to form one.

In July 2006 the Democratic leader in the Senate, Harry Reid, took the surprising step of privately urging the charismatic junior senator from Illinois, Barack Obama, to run. A number of other senators, including Tom Daschle and Hillary's colleague from New York, Chuck Schumer, also were encouraging him – privately – to do so.[27]

The Clintons were unaware of this and the betrayal, as they saw it, by colleagues they had helped by campaigning and fund-raising for them in their states came as a devastating surprise to them. Bill Clinton did understand, however, that the Democratic primaries could turn out to be a harder fight than the general election, which he was convinced Hillary would win if she was

the nominee. His concern was with the mobilisation
of the liberal wing of the party against Hillary's vote
in favour of the Iraq war.

One of her likely rivals, John Edwards, published
a recantation of his vote in favour of the war. Hillary
declined to do so. She had worked assiduously in the
Senate to get rid of her image as over-ambitious, liberal and partisan and to become regarded instead as
competent, industrious, pragmatic and centrist. She had
worked equally hard and effectively on her constituency in New York state.

She opposed in the Senate attempts to impose a bind-
ing deadline for the withdrawal of US troops from Iraq.
This she regarded as irresponsible. She was, she said,
cursed with a responsibility gene. She was not prepared
to be dragged too far to the left. She needed no convincing that Bush, Cheney and Rumsfeld had totally
mismanaged the war, but was reluctant to undercut the
military. In June 2006 she told a crowd of progressive
activists in New York that she was against Bush's open-
ended commitment, but also against a date certain for
withdrawal, provoking uproar in the hall. They also
held against her the fact that she had co-sponsored a bill
criminalising the burning of the American flag.

A few weeks earlier, she had been obliged to cope
with a front-page article in the *New York Times* about

her husband's private life. She could not credit ('This is unbelievable!') that a supposedly serious newspaper should print a front-page article based on gossip and innuendo. The early focus of the article appeared to be that the Clintons' marriage was a sham. They were rarely under the same roof together and Bill notoriously had a roving eye. As Hillary's aides weighed in with the paper, the story, when it appeared, was devoid of any facts. The public reaction was negative and the editor had to write a tortured defence of having published it at all.

The rumours, nevertheless, continued, fuelled by Bill Clinton's lifestyle and tendency to fly around the world with a Los Angeles-based friend and notorious playboy, Ron Burkle. When Hillary's team started canvassing influential figures about her political plans, they kept being asked: 'What are you going to do about Bill?' Hillary's response was that none of the rumours were true, plus anger that even her friends were raising questions of this kind.

Hardly anyone in her entourage thought seriously at the time about Obama. Hillary dismissed the idea that he would not run because he lacked experience. But he did lack a fund-raising organisation. She did not believe that much could be achieved just by words, however eloquent they might be. Bill Clinton was more wary.

Obama, though just a state senator, had voted against the war. He could present himself as representing something new.

In October 2006, Obama published his second book, *The Audacity of Hope*, and in an interview with Tim Russert, despite his previous denials, said that he was thinking about running for the Presidency.

In the mid-term elections on 8 November the Democrats routed the Republicans, re-taking control of Congress. Bill Daley, brother of the Mayor of Chicago, encouraged Obama to run, while warning him what he was up against. Hillary knew where she was going to be a year ahead (fund-raising for other Democrats), in contrast to the novice senator from Illinois.

From the outset, however, Obama was focused on the first contest, the Iowa caucuses. His advisors understood that the chances of success for him lay in getting new voters into the mix. The same applied to fund-raising, where they envisaged the broadest possible appeal, not just focused on the major donors targeted by Clinton.

At the end of the year, the former Democratic majority leader in the Senate, Tom Daschle, again pressed Obama to run. Daschle regarded Bill Clinton as duplicitous, Hillary as haughty and both of them as patronising, at any rate towards him.

Obama formally launched his campaign in Springfield,

Illinois on 10 February 2007. He understood, he said, that there was 'a certain presumption ... [an] audacity in this announcement'. He had not spent a lot of time learning the ways of Washington, 'but I have been there long enough to know that the ways of Washington must change. There are those who don't believe in talking about hope.' They wanted specific plans. There had been enough of those, 'but a shortage of hope ... It's time to turn the page.'

Hillary, meanwhile, had been holding meetings with key Democratic Party figures in New Hampshire. She was still in the midst of her re-election campaign for her Senate seat, which she was determined to win by a large majority. This she did, winning just over two-thirds of the vote. But the campaign was estimated to have cost her $35 million. Throughout it, she had remained doggedly silent about running for the Presidency, as she was bound to do. This was allowing Obama to gain momentum. Most of her advisors assumed that she would run, though not all were certain about this, until she confirmed it to them in January 2007.

Many of the key members of her campaign already were in place, following her Senate campaign. The majority were long-standing members of Hillaryland, led by her campaign manager, Patti Solis Doyle. The child of Mexican parents who settled in Chicago, she had been with Hillary since starting as her scheduler fifteen years before. Mandy Grunwald, in charge of the campaign advertisements, had been with the Clintons since 1992. The chief strategist, Mark Penn, had been helping Hillary, mainly as a pollster, for more than a decade.

In 2005 Penn had been appointed CEO of the leading public relations firm Burson Marsteller, a post which, bizarrely, he continued to hold throughout the campaign. He was cordially disliked by several of the core members of Hillaryland. He was seen by many of her long-term associates as being well to the right of most of them, a role Hillary and her husband knew she needed someone to play. He in turn regarded Solis Doyle as under-powered for the role of campaign manager (as did Bill Clinton). But no one at this time was closer to Hillary.

Hillary announced her candidacy formally on her website on 20 January 2007 (three weeks *before* Obama) saying, modishly, that she wanted to start 'a conversation with America … about your ideas and mine'. This was meant to assure everyone that she was 'listening'. She had just visited Iraq and Afghanistan, to reinforce her national security credentials, and embarked immediately on a fund-raising campaign that her team hoped would intimidate other contenders, including Obama. The polling still showed that she was regarded as a

polarising candidate, but she was confident of defeating
Senator John Edwards from Virginia, who she regarded
as a 'total phoney', and the highly promising but totally
inexperienced Barack Obama, whose speeches were high
on uplifting rhetoric, but low on content.

On 20 February 2007 the Hollywood mogul David
Geffen, along with Steven Spielberg, hosted a million-
dollar fund-raiser for Obama at the Beverly Hilton hotel
in Los Angeles. Geffen, who a few years before had
raised millions for the Clintons, had been regarded as
a personal friend and been invited more than once to
stay in the Lincoln bedroom in the White House. But
in 2005 he had declared that Hillary could not win the
Presidency. She was 'incredibly polarising … and ambition is just not a good enough reason'. The Clintons
were furious at this spectacular stab in the back.

On the eve of the Obama fund-raiser, the *New York
Times* columnist Maureen Dowd persuaded Geffen to
give her an interview about the Clintons. Dowd was a
dyed-in-the-wool Democrat, but had been appalled by
Bill Clinton's conduct and lying in the Monica Lewinsky
affair. Geffen told Dowd that Hillary would be unable
to bring the country together. Her husband was a 'reckless guy who gave his enemies a lot of ammunition to
hurt him'. He concluded by saying of the Clintons that
'everybody in politics lies but they do it with such ease,

it's troubling'. When the Hillary campaign called on him to disavow Geffen, Obama said he did not see why he should be apologising for someone else's remarks.

Bill Clinton understood earlier than others on Hillary's campaign that Obama was a different and entirely unexpected phenomenon, with her apparently unassailable lead among black voters rapidly melting away. He was infuriated by what he regarded as the fawning press coverage of Obama. The alarm bells became louder in April as the Clinton team found to their amazement that Obama was matching them in fund-raising, from a wider range of donors, in part through a well-organised small donor campaign.

The fact that the first test of electoral strength in the primaries would come in the peculiar forum of the Iowa caucuses was a major concern to the Hillary campaign. The farm states were not her natural habitat. John Edwards was ahead in the early polls and the caucus result depended on a few tens of thousands of votes from those who had bothered to sign up. Her pre-campaign visits to Iowa had left her with the impression that she had little connection with the voters there. A member of her campaign staff wrote a memo suggesting that she should by-pass Iowa. This was not a bad idea, but it was leaked immediately to the *New York Times*, rendering a side-step impossible.

She had, however, dominated the other Democratic contenders in a series of debates between April and October, showing much greater mastery of the issues, making Obama look vague and windy. Change, she argued, was 'just a word without the strength and experience to make it happen'. A poll on 30 October put her 53–20 ahead of Obama. She began to talk to her close friend Roger Altman about the issues she would face in putting together her future administration.

Obama understood that Hillary was running on inevitability. If that could be upset in Iowa, they would be into a different contest. He was continuing to perform well in raising money, including from major Los Angeles (Geffen, Edgar Bronfman) and Wall Street (Soros) donors, ahead of his campaign's web-based approach to fund-raising which was to prove so effective later. But in a debate about healthcare reform, Hillary wiped the floor with him, proving herself, not surprisingly at the time, far better informed on the issues than he was at this stage. His major supporters, the key members of his campaign team – David Axelrod, David Plouffe and Robert Gibbs – and Obama himself were increasingly concerned at his failure to dent Hillary's twenty-point lead in the polls. But Obama continued to believe that he could win Iowa.

At the time, John Edwards still was ahead in the polls

in Iowa. In October, the *National Enquirer* published details of his affair with a self-appointed publicist who was filming his campaign, but the national press had not yet picked up on this.

In an interview with the *New York Times* on 27 October, Obama had signalled his intention of going on to the offensive against Hillary, accusing her of acting like a Republican on foreign policy and of being too divisive to win a general election or unify the country. In a debate at Drexel University on 30 October, Edwards led the attack on Hillary as the candidate of big business, a throwback to the 1990s and 'more of the same'. Obama suggested that Republicans were obsessed with Hillary because 'that's a fight they are very comfortable having'. The job of the next President was to break the gridlock in Washington, to get Democrats, independents and Republicans to 'start working together to solve problems like healthcare and climate change. What we don't want is another eight years of bickering.'

The other candidates, including Joe Biden and Chris Dodd, piled in against Hillary, who declined to say whether she was for or against giving drivers' licences to illegal immigrants, as Elliot Spitzer had proposed in New York. It was the first debate she had lost and she did so comprehensively.

The press enjoyed her discomfiture: they wanted a

race, not a coronation. In a key Democratic Party rally
in Des Moines, Iowa, on 9 November, Obama's speech
and supporters upstaged Clinton's completely with his
message that 'we have the chance to bring the country
together in a new majority ... a nation healed. A world
repaired. An America that believes again.'

Hillary was increasingly alarmed at the fact that no
woman had ever been elected to Congress from Iowa
and about the peculiar nature of the Iowa caucuses at
which, it turned out, anyone – not just registered Democratic voters – could turn up to vote. She also felt that
she could not risk campaigning on the college campuses
because of her vote in favour of the Iraq war, but nor
could she afford at this stage to give up on Iowa.

Egged on by some of his own former associates who
had been excluded from Hillaryland, Bill Clinton had
developed serious doubts about the management of her
campaign and worries that Obama simply was regarded
as more likeable than her. She still was perceived as
haughty and as talking down to people, lacking the personal empathy that had been his strongest suit on the
campaign trail. The way to break Obama's momentum,
in his opinion, was to stop being statesmanlike and to
go highly negative on him.

In a chance encounter at the Reagan airport in Washington, Hillary apologised to Obama for remarks by

one of her advisors about his admitted use of drugs in his youth. When Obama complained about other insinuations about him Hillary exploded, going through the litany of Obama campaign attacks on her, leaving Obama with the impression that she was rattled. Her policy advisor, Mark Penn, said on television that they did not intend to make an issue of Obama's admitted use of cocaine! Bill Clinton, taking things into his own hands, told Charlie Rose that voters had to decide whether to roll the dice on someone who had decided to run for President after just one year as a senator.

In Iowa, on New Year's Eve, the *Des Moines Register* reported a game-changing piece of news, 'a dramatic influx of first-time caucus-goers', many of them political independents, and nearly all of them favouring Obama. In 2004, 124,000 voters had showed up. The *Register* was predicting far more than that. Over 200,000 voted, many of them for the first time in the caucuses, giving Obama a clear victory.[28]

CHAPTER 8

RUNNING AGAINST A CULT

HILLARY MOVED STRAIGHT on to the far more familiar and congenial territory to her of New Hampshire. On 5 January she was asked by a moderator why voters regarded Obama as more likeable than her. By this stage her campaign manager Patti Solis Doyle was telling her that she would lose New Hampshire and should then consider dropping out of the race, leaving Hillary tearful in a televised visit to a coffee house that evening. At Dartmouth College, Bill Clinton attacked negative propaganda from the Obama campaign about both him and his wife.

On the morning of the poll, Hillary sent Solis Doyle an email stating that it was time to make some changes. She was asked to stay on, but as deputy to Hillary's former chief of staff, Maggie Williams, who would be brought in to run the campaign. By 10 p.m. that evening, to the surprise of many of her own associates, Hillary had won a narrow victory over Obama in New Hampshire.

The focus now was on Super Tuesday, 5 February, when the primary elections were due to be held in an array of large states where Hillary's support hitherto had been strong. But, before then, Hillary had to face caucuses in Nevada and a primary in South Carolina, where 50 per cent of the Democratic electorate was African American and her campaign had run out of money.

On 9 January the *New York Times* accused the Clintons of running a campaign with racial overtones against Obama. Hillary narrowly won the popular vote in the Nevada caucuses. Given black American support for Obama, she had little prospect of doing so in South Carolina, but Bill Clinton was determined to campaign there himself. In a debate on 21 January in Myrtle Beach, South Carolina, which came to be known as the 'brawl on the beach', Obama launched a personal attack on

Hillary as 'a corporate lawyer sitting on the board at Wal-Mart', causing her to talk about his campaign contributor Rezko, who ran a slum landlord business in Chicago.

The Obama camp were worried that, in contrast to his public persona, Obama had been made to appear, as he could be in private, 'caustic, sarcastic and thin-skinned'. The effect was totally negated when, under attack by an Obama acolyte in South Carolina, a red-faced finger-wagging Bill Clinton lost his temper completely, accusing the media of falling for Obama's negative campaigning: 'Shame on you!'[29] Obama won 55 to 27 per cent in South Carolina, demonstrating that the black vote was permanently lost to Hillary.

On 27 January, despite heated efforts by Bill Clinton to dissuade him from doing so, Teddy Kennedy, reflecting the Kennedys' long-term reservations about the Clintons, who they regarded as usurpers, endorsed Obama: 'He has lit a spark of hope amid the fierce urgency of now.' Kennedy's defection brought an explosive and self-defeating reaction from Bill Clinton, who astonished a fund-raising lunch in Manhattan by listing all the favours he had done as President for Teddy Kennedy, including appointing his sister as ambassador to Ireland. Attempts by Obama to persuade Al Gore to follow suit failed, despite Gore's often fraught relationship with Hillary as, in effect, co-Vice-President in the Clinton White House. Yet on Super Tuesday Hillary won California, New Jersey, New York and, to her delight, Massachusetts, despite Teddy Kennedy's endorsement of her opponent.

But the overall popular vote was split evenly between them and, by winning more of the smaller states, Obama had ended up with slightly more delegates than Hillary. Most remarkably, Obama had developed a decisive advantage in fund-raising, aided by a web-based campaign backed by a YouTube video of the song 'Yes, We Can', a slogan based on Obama's last speech in New Hampshire. Obama won all eleven of the remaining contests in February.

Hillary was determined to fight back in Texas. She regarded Obama's speeches as resembling those of a Baptist preacher in a southern church, uplifting rhetoric devoid of content, and could not understand why the press seemed so keen to fall for this. What exactly was 'the fierce urgency of now' supposed to mean, precisely? One of her advertisements, entitled '3AM', the hour at which some crisis might require a response from the White House, challenged Obama's fitness to be commander in chief.

She was outraged by Obama's opportunistic opposition to the North American Free Trade Area, especially as one of his associates was caught telling the Canadian government that this was purely tactical. She declared that she had a lifetime of experience to bring to the White House. So did Senator McCain. 'And Senator Obama has a speech he made in 2002.' Running now as the underdog, she won Texas narrowly and Ohio by a wider margin.

On 13 March the Obama campaign suffered a serious setback when his pastor and friend in Chicago, the Reverend Jeremiah Wright, who had married the Obamas, was revealed by *ABC News* to have ranted about the treatment of black Americans, who, he suggested, instead of singing 'God Bless America' should say 'God-damn America.'

Obama hastily dictated a statement that these remarks were 'inflammatory and appalling'. Barack Obama had in fact lifted the title of *The Audacity of Hope* from one of Wright's sermons. In a masterstroke, he responded with his most serious and thoughtful speech of the campaign in Philadelphia on 18 March, about race relations and entitled 'A More Perfect Union'. It led Michelle Obama to make the unfortunate statement that 'for the first time in my adult lifetime, I'm really proud of my country'.

Hillary was suffering woes of her own over a story she had been telling in the campaign about arriving in

Bosnia as First Lady in 1996 under sniper fire, racing across the tarmac with her head down. In fact by then the war was over and a video surfaced of her and Chelsea being greeted at Tuzla airport by a group of cheering children. Nevertheless, she defeated Obama easily in Pennsylvania. On 6 May Obama won North Carolina, with its large black electorate, easily, and came within a point of defeating Hillary in Indiana.

Hillary came back in West Virginia, but was by now on life support. She caused a rumpus by telling *USA Today* that Obama's support among 'working, hard-working Americans, white Americans' was weakening again. In Sioux Falls, ahead of the South Dakota primary on 3 June, her exhaustion contributed to her making an unbelievable gaffe. She did not, she said, understand the calls for her to give up. Her husband had not won the 1992 nomination until June and 'we all remember Bobby Kennedy was assassinated in June in California'.

Hillary faced the press to tell them that she had meant only to stress the unpredictability of long campaigns. She won South Dakota, but Obama, by winning Montana and securing sufficient votes from the so-called 'super-delegates', elected to the convention on the basis that they could vote for whichever candidate they chose, had clinched the nomination, bumping fists with his wife to celebrate.

*   *   *

On 5 June 2008, lying on the back seat of a minivan to avoid the reporters staking out her home in Washington, Hillary set off for a meeting with Barack Obama at the house of Senator Dianne Feinstein, who left the two of them alone to talk together. Obama told her, not to her surprise, that he was unlikely to pick her as his running mate, a position she claimed not to want anyway. He asked for her help and that of her husband in re-uniting the Democratic Party and winning the Presidency.

On the following day, she held a wake with her exhausted and bitterly disappointed campaign staff, but made clear that she would be giving Obama her whole-hearted support. On 7 June, in a valedictory speech in Washington, she told her supporters: 'Although we weren't able to shatter that highest, hardest glass ceiling this time, thanks to you, it's got about eighteen million cracks in it.' The eighteen million votes she had received were very nearly as many as Obama, who won the nomination by polling just 150,000 votes more than her. She acknowledged that the night she lost the Iowa caucuses to Obama had been 'excruciating'. She came out of the experience realising, she believed, that she no longer cared so much what the critics said about her.

On 27 June they made a joint appearance at the

carefully chosen venue of Unity, New Hampshire. Reflecting on her campaign, Hillary told her supporters that they had the entire press corps against her, with a total free ride for Obama. It was hard to run against an African American when much of the Democratic establishment were scared of opposing him. Then there was 'the Oprah thing'. The Obama movement had been more like a cult than a campaign.

Barack Obama, who at the outset had pledged campaign finance reform, dropped that idea like a hot potato as he found that his web-based fund-raising would far exceed the $8 million his Republican opponent, Senator John McCain, would secure from public funds.

At the Democratic convention in Denver in August, both the Clintons made speeches wholeheartedly endorsing Obama. Not content with making his own speech, Bill Clinton tried to edit Hillary's, causing her to snap, 'It's *my* speech.' Over the next few weeks, the Clintons attended a hundred events and fund-raisers in support of the Obama campaign.[30]

John McCain, meanwhile, astonished his party and the world by choosing the wholly untested Governor of Alaska, Sarah Palin, as his running mate. He had been told that his original choice, the right-wing Democrat senator Joe Lieberman, would have caused a revolt at the Republican convention. McCain barely knew Palin and the vetting was flimsy and haphazard. His choice was seen as both high risk and reckless by many of his fellow Republicans. She manifestly was incredibly unprepared to take over if anything should happen to the 72-year-old senator. Nevertheless, at the Republican convention she scored a success with a speech labelling Obama an elitist, a taxer, a spender, an appeaser and an accomplishment-free zone.

The continuing implosion of Wall Street came to the aid of the Obama campaign as, in September, Lehman Brothers sought bankruptcy protection. An ill-judged descent on Washington by John McCain in the midst of the bail-out crisis backfired, as he clearly was out of touch, while Obama was sounding statesmanlike.

In the first presidential debate, Obama pointed out how wrong McCain had proven to be about weapons of mass destruction and the US being regarded as liberators in Iraq. The Obama campaign had a huge advantage in fund-raising and McCain had not fared well, looking old and negative, in the second and third presidential debates. General Colin Powell, a long-term friend of McCain, ended up endorsing Obama. Obama by then had built an unassailable lead. On 4 November, he won the election with 53 per cent of the vote (95–4 among African Americans, 66–32 among Hispanic voters and 43 per cent of white Americans).

Obama's campaign team knew that he had been considering Hillary Clinton for a senior role in his administration. Most of them were opposed to this. They feared that she would seek to be a rival centre of power in his administration. Obama, however, had learned grudgingly to admire her toughness, resilience and staying power.

On 13 November, they met at Obama's office in Chicago. She expected to be offered some post as a unifying gesture, but not that of Secretary of State. Obama certainly calculated that, with her in his administration, this would conjure away the danger of any primary challenge to him in 2011.

Her instinctive reaction was to refuse. She did not want to play second fiddle to the new President. She was exhausted and wanted her own life back. She had no idea at this stage whether Obama in his first term would succeed or fail and wanted to keep her options open. Had he thought, she said, of appointing her friend Dick Holbrooke, or Senator George Mitchell?

Everyone else felt that she should accept, including Bill Clinton. But Hillary remained adamant. On 19 November, Obama's staff were told that she had decided to reject his offer. At midnight, she was telephoned by Obama. She told him that she was exhausted and had $6 million of debt to pay down, which she could not do as Secretary of State.

Obama said that the economy was in a much bigger mess than he had imagined and he was going to have to focus on that for the next two years. He talked about the challenge posed by the wars in Iraq and Afghanistan and by Iran and North Korea. He needed her as Secretary of State. Her husband's role could be managed. He would not take no for an answer. 'Don't say no to me.' He wanted her to sleep on it.

Sleep on it she did. She had signed off a statement conveying her 'deep appreciation' for his offer, but concluding that her place was in the Senate. By next morning, she had decided to accept Obama's offer, presented extravagantly by some of the press as being an attempt to re-create Jefferson's 'Team of Rivals', Jefferson having appointed William Henry Seward as his Secretary of State, after having defeated him for the Republican nomination.

CHAPTER 9

'WHY DON'T YOU PIVOT OUT OF HERE?'

T O PERSUADE HILLARY to serve as his Secretary of State, to the dismay of his advisors, Obama had agreed that she could make most of the key appointments to senior posts in the State Department, though not that of deputy secretary or senior ambassadors.

Hillary's key aide in making these appointments was Cheryl Mills, who was appointed as both chief of staff and counsellor to Hillary, dealing with Denis

McDonough on Obama's team. Mills had served in the White House counsel's office during Bill Clinton's impeachment hearings and as legal counsellor during Hillary's election campaign. She could be relied upon to defend Hillary's territory with sharp elbows.

Hillary's other closest aide throughout her time in Foggy Bottom was Huma Abedin. The intensely loyal and efficient Abedin, a Muslim daughter of South Asian immigrants, had played the same role for her in the Senate. Hillary's *modus operandi* was one in which authority flowed essentially from proximity to her. Huma's authority stemmed from the fact that everyone knew she was closer than anyone to Hillary.

Hillary's close friend and foreign policy advisor, Richard Holbrooke, had hoped to become deputy Secretary of State. Obama's team, however, had not forgotten the messages he had left on the phones of various foreign policy figures threatening to bar them from jobs in the Clinton administration if they helped Obama. Obama's choice was Jim Steinberg, who had served as deputy national security advisor under Bill Clinton and as an advisor to Obama during the campaign. The reliable, low-profile Steinberg was acceptable to Hillary, but she appointed a Citigroup banker, Jack Lew, as a second deputy to her, with responsibility for management and the budget.

Within the Bush State Department Bill Burns, the under-secretary for political affairs, was the highest-ranking career foreign service officer. Briefing Hillary in December, he made a sufficient impression to convince her that she should keep him on in the post. Burns told her that a 'little bit of attention' would go a very long way with the hardworking, dedicated and often under-appreciated career State Department staff.

This was a message Hillary did not forget, becoming one of the most popular Secretaries within the Department of the modern era. She decided also to continue the appointment of Pat Kennedy as the under-secretary for management.

Hillary by now was preparing for her confirmation hearings. Although certain to be a shoo-in, characteristically she devoted a vast amount of time and effort to preparing for these.

Hillary saw it as her objective to restore America's standing in the world, damaged as it had been, she was convinced, by the arbitrary actions, disregard for the views of others and excessive reliance on military force by George W. Bush, Cheney and Rumsfeld. She wanted instead to infuse the modish idea of 'smart power' into US foreign policy. The term had been popularised by the Harvard professor Joe Nye, who had declared that smart power was 'neither hard nor soft. It is both.'[31] It was supposed to rely on a more sophisticated approach to foreign nations, offering them diplomatic, economic and political incentives to cooperate with the United States. Hillary declared that she wanted 'an America that was going to protect its interests but could take into account the concerns and perspectives of others as well'.

Richard Holbrooke, architect of the Dayton Accords that had ended the Bosnian war, was appointed as her special representative for Afghanistan and Pakistan. The former senator George Mitchell was appointed special envoy to the Middle East, giving him the thankless task of dealing with the Israelis and Palestinians and, crucially, putting some distance between that problem and her. Another veteran of successive administrations, Dennis Ross, became her counsellor on Iran. Unsurprisingly, there was no post in the department for Samantha Power, an advisor to Obama, who had called Hillary 'a monster' in the course of the campaign. She ended up on the NSC staff instead. Susan Rice, who, on behalf of Obama, also had attacked Hillary during the campaign, became US ambassador to the United Nations. Despite the prior frictions, they cooperated effectively together on sanctions against Iran and North Korea.

Hillary had been at pains to consult every previous Secretary of State, including Henry Kissinger, who considered 'smart power' to be a banal idea, but had a

healthy respect for her. She got on well with her immediate predecessor, Condoleezza (Condi) Rice. She made
the necessary pilgrimage to hear the views of every one
of her former Senate colleagues who wanted to see her
before the formal hearings. The *New York Times*, still
pursuing what many felt had become a vendetta against
Hillary, urged the Senate foreign affairs committee to
examine the 'awkward intersection between Mrs Clinton's new post and the charitable and business activities
of her husband'.[32]

After six hours of mainly friendly questioning, two
Tea Party-aligned Republican senators, David Vitter and
Jim DeMint, were the sole dissenting voices. She was
confirmed by the full Senate 94–2. An emotional farewell reunion with her Senate colleagues was attended
by a number of friends she had made across the aisle,
notably the Republican senators Susan Collins, Lindsey Graham, John McCain and Olympia Snowe. In a
bizarre speech, the Senate majority leader, Harry Reid,
who had backed Obama to the hilt against her, declared
that 'parting is such sweet sorrow. I feel like crying.'[33]

Finally arriving in Foggy Bottom on 22 January 2009,
Hillary was greeted as a celebrity, with whoops, cheers,
flashing cameras and hopes that she would do something
to restore the battered prestige of the department. While
clashes continued between their staffs, Hillary insisted

on proper deference to Obama as President. Because of the long and bitter primary battle, she knew that the press would be looking – and hoping – for signs of disagreement between them. She intended to deprive them of such stories and did so with iron discipline throughout her four years as Secretary of State.

In an early bureaucratic victory, she insisted that the 'Strategic Economic Dialogue' that Tim Geithner and the Treasury were seeking to develop with China should be broadened into a 'Strategic and Economic Dialogue' in which she and her department would be involved.

When the head of the Office for Management and the Budget, Peter Orszag, tried to inflict a cut in the State Department budget, as he was doing with other departments, Hillary sent his predecessor in the office, Jack Lew, to tell him that this was unacceptable. The dispute was escalated to the President. With the support of Bob Gates as Defense Secretary, Hillary got the increase she wanted.

Within the National Security Council, Gates, who had served in eight administrations, was the only member whose experience was anything like, indeed superior to, hers. Gates had been re-appointed by Obama as Defense Secretary, having served in that position for two years under George W. Bush. Although they barely knew each other until this point, Gates soon found

Hillary, whose hawkish views had cost her during the election campaign, his closest ally within the new administration. They got quickly into the habit of concerting their views before national security meetings, with Hillary far more respectful of the military than the Vice-President, Joe Biden. They were a powerful tandem, periodically lunching together, particularly as the national security advisor at this stage, the former NATO commander General Jim Jones, was never an Obama intimate. Hillary prided herself on the fact that neither would tolerate the traditional infighting between the State Department and the Pentagon.[34]

*   *   *

Hillary was conscious of a drumbeat from some of the Washington think tanks that America was in relative decline, a view also expressed by experts on Obama's National Intelligence Council, given what they called the 'historic transfer of relative wealth and economic power from West to East'. The Yale historian Professor Paul Kennedy was another exponent of this view, rejected by Hillary as under-estimating America's capacity for innovation and renewal. Both she and Obama, who had grown up in Indonesia and Hawaii, did believe, however, that the moment had come for what they declared to be a 'pivot towards Asia'. Hillary's first overseas visit as Secretary of State was to Japan, Indonesia, South Korea and China. The 'pivot' was formally publicised by her in an article she wrote subsequently in *Foreign Policy*.[35]

When North Korea in May 2009 performed an underground nuclear test and denounced the 1953 armistice with South Korea, she managed to persuade the Chinese Foreign Minister to agree to some additional sanctions. To rescue two women reporters with US nationality who had been sentenced to hard labour in North Korea, Bill Clinton was despatched, successfully, to Pyongyang.

She regarded China as 'the epicentre of the antidemocratic movement in Asia',[36] arguing in her speeches around the region that democracy was the right choice for everyone and that they could not have economic without political liberalisation, a theory the Chinese remained, and remain, determined to disprove. During her February 2009 visit, the Chinese complained to her that the US had no plans to build a pavilion at the 2011 Shanghai Exposition. Hillary used her fund-raising contacts, led by her friend Elizabeth Bagley, to raise the money needed for a fashionably 'carbon neutral' US pavilion, visited by the Chinese President, Hu Jintao, and seven million of his compatriots. Hillary felt that she had lived up to her billing for getting things done.

In November 2009, however, Obama received a very

lukewarm reception in what had been billed as a 'G2' visit to Beijing. The Americans were concerned at signs of increasing assertiveness by the Chinese in the South and East China seas, the scene of a jumble of competing territorial claims between China, Japan, Vietnam and the Philippines. In May 2010, Hillary had to listen to a rant by a Chinese admiral who accused the US of trying to encircle China. At a regional meeting in Hanoi, her call for a multilateral solution got a hostile reception from the Chinese Foreign Minister Yang. Her favourite Chinese official, Dai Bingguo, told her: 'Why don't you pivot out of here?'[37] Her book *Hard Choices* is not being translated in China and access to it is being made difficult there.

In April 2012 a blind Chinese dissident, Chen Guangcheng, escaped from house arrest in his province and asked for refuge at the US embassy in Beijing. Hillary authorised him to be picked up by an embassy car. As she arrived on a further visit, the Chinese agreed to Chen's demand that he should study at a Chinese university, though he first was taken to a local hospital. He immediately campaigned via the western media to be allowed to leave for the US, with Hillary being attacked for, supposedly, obliging him to leave the embassy. Following further remonstrances, Chen was allowed to leave China. The case was a massive distraction from

her talks with the Chinese leaders about Iran and North
Korea, but Hillary regarded it as being about 'the human
rights and aspirations of more than a billion people here
in China'.

*   *   *

Hillary described meeting Aung San Suu Kyi in December 2011 as one of her most moving experiences. 'We
just started talking like we were old friends.' Aung San
Suu Kyi said that she wanted to become a 'real flesh
and blood politician'.

There was a lot of scepticism that the military regime
really was prepared to liberalise, but Suu Kyi had been
released and Hillary mobilised support from key senators for a graduated US response to further reforms. She
and Suu Kyi stayed in touch by telephone in the following months, as she and forty of her colleagues were
elected to the Burmese parliament. In September 2012,
Aung San Suu Kyi visited the US. The reform process
was continuing, sanctions were being eased and the US
and Burma exchanged ambassadors. In her public statements, Hillary compared her to Nelson Mandela. In
November 2012, immediately following her re-election,
Obama and Hillary made their last overseas trip together
to meet the Burmese government and Suu Kyi.[38]

Bill and Hillary at Yale, 1971

Getting married. Little Rock, 11 October 1975

Hillary standing by her man

'Two for the price of one.' The President and First Lady conferring together, September 1996

Debating against Obama in Charleston, South Carolina, July 2007

A hug for Obama on passing the Affordable Health Care Act, May 2010

Hillary and Aung San Suu Kyi, December 2011

This picture 'does capture how I felt': watching the raid to kill bin Laden,
1 May 2011

Sharing a joke with Angela Merkel, June 2011

'I love you, darling!' Hillary and Vice-President Joe Biden, January 2009

Hillary partying in Cartagena, Colombia, April 2012

Despite the progress in Burma, which fell a long way short of Aung San Suu Kyi taking over there, the 'pivot to Asia' could hardly be accounted a success. The attempt to co-opt China as a principal partner of the US in solving the world's problems was dismissed by the Chinese, though they did agree to some additional sanctions against Iran and North Korea and not to veto the western intervention in Libya. That, however, was as far as they were prepared to go.

They were deeply suspicious of US ambitions in the Pacific and the temptation for the US to intervene in the disputes with all their neighbours in the East and South China seas. The dispute over Chinese activities in the Paracel Islands off the coast of Vietnam was to lead to anti-Chinese demonstrations in Hanoi. After Hillary left office, her deputy for Asia, Kurt Campbell, believed that he had agreed with the Chinese on a mutual withdrawal of Chinese and Philippine vessels from the Spratly Islands, disputed between them, only for the Chinese vessels then to fail to withdraw. This led President Aquino of the Philippines and other regional states to question how much US support was worth in resisting continuing Chinese aggressive actions in the South China Sea. The very hard-boiled Defence Minister of a key US ally in the region asked me if I had any idea to what extent the Obama administration could be counted on from this point of view. I said that I did not but, far more worryingly, nor did he. If Hillary does get to the White House, she is going to have to embark on a fresh campaign to reassure the United States' key allies in Asia.

CHAPTER 10

THE 'RE-SET' WITH RUSSIA

F OR HER SECOND visit abroad, Hillary flew to Geneva in March 2009 for a first meeting with the Russian Foreign Minister, Sergey Lavrov. Her ambition, and that of Obama, was to 're-set' the relationship with Russia, which they considered had become far too adversarial under George W. Bush. She took with her to the meeting a green box, complete with a ribbon. In front of the cameras, she opened it and presented Lavrov with a bright red button on a yellow base with the Russian word 'peregruzka'. Lavrov politely explained that they had got the translation wrong. The Russian word for 're-set' was 'perezagruzka'. 'This means "overcharged"', he said.

Her press secretary, Philippe Reines, tried to get the gift back to change the label, saying that otherwise his boss was going to send him to Siberia. It was, she admitted, a tempting thought, but Reines survived as, to this day, one of her closest advisors.[39]

Obama and Hillary had a first meeting with Dmitry Medvedev, who had taken over from Putin as President, at the US ambassador's residence in London in April 2009. Putin had swapped jobs to become Prime Minister, but Medvedev had surprised people by bringing a new, more conciliatory tone to the Kremlin. Hillary had been a critic of Putin, but regarded it as counterproductive to see Russia only as a threat when there were issues on which Russia and the US needed to cooperate, and Medvedev did not have Putin's Cold War and KGB history.

Obama and Medvedev discussed a new treaty cutting nuclear weapons. On Afghanistan, Medvedev agreed to facilitate US supply routes, which was important, as the US otherwise was entirely dependent on Pakistan. He acknowledged that Russia had under-estimated Iran's nuclear ambitions, eventually supporting a vote at the UN to impose tougher sanctions, despite Russia's own civil nuclear cooperation with Iran. He continued to oppose US plans for missile defence in Europe, despite US assurances that this was directed at Iran, not Russia. Obama promised support for Russia's admission to the World Trade Organization.

A broken elbow caused her to miss Obama's subsequent visit to Moscow in July, when he and Medvedev issued a joint statement on terrorism, advanced work on the new nuclear arms treaty and sought to find some common ground on Iran and North Korea. An agreement was formally signed to allow the transit of US military equipment through Russia to Afghanistan.

The new strategic arms reduction treaty ('New START') was signed in April 2010. Hillary and Biden led the campaign to secure the two-thirds majority needed to get it ratified by the Senate, helped by the co-chairman of the foreign relations committee, John Kerry, for the Democrats and the moderate Republican Richard Lugar. She spoke to eighteen senators, nearly all of them Republicans, in helping to get the treaty ratified by seventy-one votes to twenty-six. Gates regarded the White House (but not Hillary) as naïve about the 're-set'. He pointed out to Obama that on the day the treaty was signed, the Russians were practising a mock nuclear attack on the United States ('a nice Putin touch!').[40]

The successes of the relationship that had developed

with Medvedev included imposing stronger sanctions on Iran and North Korea and winning Russian acceptance of the no-fly zone in Libya. But in September 2011 Medvedev announced that Putin would run again for President in the following year. At a conference in Lithuania, Hillary denounced the harassment of opposition groups in the Russian parliamentary elections, thereby contributing, in Putin's view, to demonstrations against him ('she gave them a signal').

In May 2012, Putin returned as President and forthwith declined Obama's invitation to a G8 summit at Camp David. Hillary told Obama that Putin was deeply resentful and suspicious of the US. His declared ambition of 'regional integration' was code for the reassertion of Russian dominance over the 'near abroad'. In Syria, the Russians propped up the Assad regime and blocked all attempts at the UN to organise an international response. Putin resumed threatening Ukraine and started re-opening old military bases and becoming assertive in the Arctic. Visiting Georgia (twice), Hillary further annoyed him by calling on Russia to end its occupation of the territory it had seized in 2008.[41]

To Hillary, therefore, the Russian seizure of Crimea came as no surprise, but simply as the opportunist pursuit by Putin of his long-standing aims – and a serious wake-up call. She compared Putin's seizure of Crimea and intervention in eastern Ukraine to Hitler's tactics in Sudetenland. Following the halting of gas exports to Ukraine in January 2009, when Hillary met EU leaders in March, she had urged joint actions to reduce European dependence on Russian gas, including promoting the 'southern corridor' pipeline from the Caspian.

Hillary believes that the feeble response to the annexation of Crimea emboldened Putin to intervene aggressively in eastern Ukraine. It took the shooting down of the Malaysian Airlines aircraft to produce a more united western response. She will remain concerned at the failure of the Europeans as yet to do much about reducing their dependence on Russia and their continuing very low level of defence spending.

As for Putin, at a dinner in Vladivostok, he told Hillary the horrifying story of his father rescuing his mother from a pile of bodies outside their destroyed apartment building during the German siege of Leningrad, only to find that she was still, just about, alive. In a valedictory memo to Obama, she warned again that Putin saw the US primarily as a competitor and the contest between them as a zero-sum game.[42] She also, however, described him as running scared of domestic opposition, seriously over-estimating the extent of opposition to him.

The final offence, so far as Hillary is concerned, is

the asylum given by Putin to Edward Snowden, the
National Security Agency (NSA) contractor whose
leaked material, far more serious than that of WikiLeaks, revealed some of America's most closely guarded
intelligence programmes monitoring the activities of terrorists world-wide. She accepts that the US should not
have been monitoring Angela Merkel's mobile phone
calls (though everyone else was),[43] but Edward Snowden
would be extremely unwise ever to count on a presidential pardon from Hillary.

CHAPTER 11

'AF-PAK'

BEFORE BEING SWORN in as Secretary of State, Hillary had sought out General David Petraeus, who was credited with the success of the military 'surge' which had stabilised the situation in Iraq. As they were to confess later, both Hillary and Obama had opposed the 'surge' for electoral reasons at the time. Petraeus was now head of Central Command, overseeing the conflict in Afghanistan.

Hillary wanted him to work with Holbrooke, who was convinced of the need for a similar military surge there as the only way, he hoped, to bring the Taliban to the negotiating table. During the campaign, both Obama and Hillary had argued for an increase in forces in Afghanistan, accusing the Bush administration of neglecting that conflict as against the one in Iraq. As President, Obama made an initial commitment of 21,000 more troops for Afghanistan, pending a decision about a larger increase in forces to be made later.

This led to a series of acrimonious and inconclusive NSC meetings, with Joe Biden wanting a draw-down rather than an increase in US forces, as did Obama's key domestic advisors, Rahm Emmanuel and David Axelrod. Hillary had visited Afghanistan three times as a senator. She did not see how the US could disengage without first doing all it could to bolster the ability of the Afghan regime and forces to cope by themselves and wanted to intensify the civilian side of the US effort there. Like Gates, she was sceptical that it would be possible to achieve a diplomatic outcome between Karzai, the Taliban and Pakistan. But she wanted an 'Af-Pak' strategy that concentrated also on Pakistan's role in the conflict.

Holbrooke's abrasive personality and quest for publicity grated on Obama, despite Hillary's protection of him. He also fell out terminally with President Karzai, openly supporting opposition politicians against him in the 2009 Afghan elections, as did the US ambassador,

Karl Eikenberg. General Jones's influence was eclipsed
progressively by two key Obama staffers, Tom Donilon
and Denis McDonough, who, in turn, were to succeed
him as national security advisor.

Bob Gates found the protracted inconclusive discussions about force levels in Afghanistan a dispiriting and
frustrating experience, an opinion shared by the CIA
director, Leon Panetta. Gates was infuriated by the attitude of the Vice-President, Joe Biden, who he regarded
as having been wrong on every national security issue he
could think of in the past twenty years. But he had nothing but praise for Hillary as, in his view, a serious team
player who understood that the US could not just walk
away. They had to try to maintain stability in Afghanistan. Biden, who had had a series of rows with Karzai,
on one occasion storming out of a dinner with him,
kept warning the President against being 'bullied'
by the military and that any increase in troops, whatever
the military reasons, would be intolerable politically.[44]

In June the new US commander in Afghanistan, General McChrystal, who had led the counter-insurgency
operations in Iraq, reported that the military situation was
worse than he had expected and started signalling that he
was going to ask for more troops. Biden's approach of
relying mainly on drone strikes would not, in McChrystal's view, work without effective military support.

Hillary and Gates both wanted the US ambassador in Kabul, Eikenberg, replaced as his relationship with Karzai was so poor, but he was protected by the White House. Gates was appalled to find that, whereas the entire NSC staff under Bush numbered forty-five, under Obama twenty-five NSC staffers were working on Afghanistan, all bent, in Gates's view, on second-guessing the commanders in the field.

On 26 October 2009 in a meeting with the President, Hillary supported Gates's recommendation of 30,000 more troops, arguing that this offered no guarantee of success, but the alternative virtually guaranteed failure. She told Obama that the Iraq surge had worked. Her opposition to it had been because she was facing him in the Iowa primary. Obama 'conceded vaguely' that his opposition to the surge also had been political. Gates professed to be shocked by these comments. With the President and her together in Asia, Gates again enlisted Hillary's support. Obama by now was resigned to sending 30,000 more troops, coupled with an announcement that the troop levels would be drawn down from July 2011. Hillary realised that this clearly was liable to be self-defeating as a message to the Taliban. It was a 'starker deadline' than she had hoped for and she worried that it might send the wrong message to friend and foe. But that was the basis on which the decision was announced, leaving Gates 'fed up' with the White House staff and the entire process.[45]

She found dealing with the Afghan President, Hamid Karzai, intensely frustrating. He was proud, stubborn and quick to bristle at any perceived slight, leading to frequent fits of temper and public attacks on his US allies. At times, he appeared to be blaming the Americans more than the Taliban for the violence in his country. Hillary found this hard to stomach, given the sacrifices US troops were making. Nor did he see the Taliban as his primary opponent in the war. That role, in his eyes, was reserved for Pakistan.

Still, as Hillary observed, 'we needed him'. Unlike Biden, Holbrooke and Eikenberg, she was unfailingly patient, respectful and courteous in her dealings with him. In the August 2009 elections, in which he was convinced Holbrooke was plotting to get rid of him, she persuaded him to agree to a second-round runoff against his main competitor, Abdullah, who, however, then withdrew. He failed utterly to deal with rampant corruption, including the looting of the Kabul Bank. She was horrified when Karzai signed a law virtually eliminating the rights of women from the Shia minority to bolster his support with its leaders, and managed to get some amendments made to it.[46]

While Karzai was willing to flirt with anyone claiming

to represent the Taliban, he was adamantly against the Americans doing so. Holbrooke and others hoped that they could be induced to distance themselves permanently from Al Qaeda, though a formal inter-agency intelligence assessment led by the experienced CIA analyst Bruce Riedel had concluded that the Taliban leaders were 'not reconcilable' and the US could not make a deal that included them.

In March 2010 Obama made his first visit to Afghanistan. In his meeting with Karzai, he pressed him on corruption and the regime's continuing involvement in drug-trafficking. On Obama's return, Gates told him of his concerns about the US ambassador, Eikenberg, who remained in a state of open war with Karzai. According to Bob Gates, Hillary attended a meeting with him and General Jones 'loaded for bear' about the NSC staff's back channel to Eikenberg. If they wanted control of the civilian side of the war, she threatened, she would hand it over to them.[47] McChrystal, who got on better with Karzai, felt that the White House was simply not behind the military campaign. Karzai, however, was on his best behaviour during a visit to Washington in May.

On 21 June, Gates was told that *Rolling Stone* magazine was about to publish an article entitled 'The Runaway General' about the McChrystal team's views on the White House and the war. These were that the

President did not seem very engaged, that the NSC advisor, General Jones, was a clown and that McChrystal had a similar view of Vice-President Biden. Obama, understandably, decided to dismiss McChrystal, and to appoint General Petraeus to succeed him. In October, General Jones was replaced as national security advisor by Tom Donilon, who, for a time at least, was much closer to the President.

Gates and Hillary were infuriated by a disparaging assessment by Doug Lute of the NSC staff of the US effort in Afghanistan. Both objected to the NSC staff, as they saw it, conducting its own foreign policy. In an assessment of corruption in Afghanistan, with Hillary distinguishing between corruption that was 'endemic' and corruption that was 'predatory', both questioned US payments to key Afghan officials, but 'ran into a stone wall called Panetta' (head of the CIA).[48]

In July 2010, Hillary visited Islamabad for the signing of a US-brokered transit trade agreement between Afghanistan and Pakistan. She was well aware that elements of the Pakistani intelligence service (ISI) had close relationships with the Taliban dating from the struggle against the Soviet occupation in the 1980s. They continued to provide safe havens for them in Pakistan and to support the insurgency as a way to pressurise the Afghan government and as a hedge against Indian influence in Kabul.

In a series of visits, she kept trying to get the Pakistan government to see the war in Afghanistan as a shared responsibility and to deny the Taliban access to their safe havens in the border regions.

*   *   *

Hillary paints an affectionate picture of her (and my) bulldozer friend, Richard Holbrooke, architect of the Dayton Accords that ended the war in Bosnia. His tactics on that occasion had included walking the Serb leader, Slobodan Milošević, through a gigantic hangar at the Wright-Paterson air force base full of US warplanes. He had long been a Hillary favourite, working with her on the campaign against AIDS.

She admitted that his style took some getting used to, pitching his ideas relentlessly, phoning her again and again, walking into meetings uninvited, 'even once following me into a ladies restroom so that he could finish making his point – in Pakistan no less'. The White House staff could not stand him. She found it painful to watch their intrigues against him. Asked to get rid of him, she refused, unless instructed to do so by the President himself.

On 11 December 2010, in a meeting in her office, he collapsed in devastating fashion with a torn aorta. She rushed to the hospital but, two days later, Holbrooke died. She went out that evening to the Ritz Carlton hotel with a large group of his friends for an impromptu wake, with everyone swapping their favourite Holbrooke stories. At the memorial service in Washington, Hillary observed that there were few people who could say that they had stopped a war.[49] Obama delivered a cautious eulogy.

*   *   *

By March 2011 Biden again was calling for a dramatic reduction in US forces in Afghanistan. Petraeus had annoyed Obama by telling NATO that the handover to Afghans would 'commence' in 2014. Obama wanted the drawdown accelerated rather than delayed, adding, 'If I believe I am being gamed…' Gates thought to himself: 'The President doesn't trust his commander, can't stand Karzai, doesn't believe in his own strategy and doesn't consider the war to be his. For him, it's all about getting out,' with Biden egging him on.[50] Gates asked the National Security Council whether the objective was to get out of Afghanistan at all costs or to achieve some measure of success for the President and the US. Biden wanted all the surge forces withdrawn by April 2012. Gates was arguing for them to stay through a further summer campaign.

Gates told Obama that he knew he wanted to end the war, but how he ended it would be of crucial importance. Gates observed that during the campaign Obama had denounced Iraq as a bad war, based on a false premise (the existence of weapons of mass destruction), while calling for a greater effort to be made in Afghanistan. Once in office, however, he did not really want to be in Afghanistan either, though nor did he want to have to hand it back, on his watch, to the Taliban.

Hillary Clinton argued forcefully in support of Gates. Obama pressed for the surge troops to be withdrawn by July. Leon Panetta told Obama that Defense, State and the CIA all were recommending that they should stay until September. This time they were supported by Donilon and McDonough. Obama announced the withdrawal of 10,000 'surge' troops in December 2011 and the remainder at the end of summer 2012.

*   *   *

Following the successful operation to kill bin Laden, described in the Prologue, Hillary and Gates had to deal with the fallout. Pakistan was in uproar about the violation of its sovereignty, but Zardari was philosophical. He saw himself as fighting the people who had killed his wife, but Hillary was firm that 'we want greater cooperation'.

Six months later, a far more serious crisis erupted when twenty-four Pakistani soldiers were killed by US forces in an operation on the Afghan border. In retaliation, Pakistan closed the supply routes to the NATO forces in Afghanistan. The Pakistanis wanted a public apology. This was resisted by the White House, the Pentagon and the CIA, all of whom felt that the Pakistanis had a good deal to apologise for themselves. The White House staff feared that any apology by Obama would be exploited against him by the Republican candidate in the 2012 presidential election, Mitt Romney.

In this absurd situation, Hillary offered to take any incoming flak herself. She despatched Tom Nides, who had taken over from Jack Lew as one of her deputies, to negotiate a carefully worded apology: 'We are sorry for the losses suffered by the Pakistani military. We are committed to working closely with Pakistan and Afghanistan to prevent this from ever happening again.'[51] Pakistan had been suffering financially from the closure of the supply routes, which were now re-opened.

*　　*　　*

In 2010, the Americans had identified a Taliban contact, Syed Tayyab Agha, who appeared to want to talk to them. The Americans wanted the Taliban to make a public statement dissociating themselves from Al Qaeda. The Taliban wanted to be allowed to open a political office in Qatar. Karzai was suspicious of these contacts and Afghan officials leaked Agha's identity to the press. When contacts resumed, Karzai professed to be in favour of them. Hillary had managed to replace Eikenberg with an experienced ambassador, Ryan Crocker, with whom Karzai was on good terms. Agha produced what he claimed to be a letter from Mullah Omar to Obama; the Americans were uncertain whether Mullah Omar was still alive. But at a conference on Afghanistan in Bonn in December 2011, Karzai berated the Americans for failing to keep him informed and insisted on having his own representatives involved in the talks, causing Agha to withdraw.

In January 2013, just before leaving office, Hillary had dinner with Karzai in Washington, urging him to stick to his commitment to abide by the Afghan constitution and not to stand again for President in 2014. She urged him to agree to the Taliban being allowed to open an office in Qatar.

In June 2013, after she left the State Department, what had been intended to be the Taliban representative office opened in Qatar. The Taliban immediately declared it to represent the 'Islamic Republic of Afghanistan', causing a furious reaction from Karzai. As the Taliban refused to give way, the office was closed. Riedel so far had turned out to be right. But Hillary had no regrets at having supported Holbrooke's effort to try to engage with the Taliban.

*   *   *

The further debate over force levels in Afghanistan was Gates's last battle in the Obama administration. In July 2011 he resigned, having recommended Leon Panetta to succeed him. He had found the Obama White House to be the most controlling of any he had worked under since that of Nixon and Henry Kissinger. The Obama White House staff had a far greater role in national security decision-making than he had ever known before. Gates resented and resisted NSC staff member attempts to deal direct with the field commanders. 'The controlling nature of the Obama White House, and the determination to take credit for every good thing that happened while giving none to people in the cabinet departments – in the trenches – who had actually done the work, offended Hillary Clinton as much as it did me.' Throughout his memoirs, Gates gives high praise to Hillary, as a good ally, supporting him on difficult issues, despite their disagreement over Libya.[52]

She in turn proved herself to be a good soldier from

another point of view. Although she shared Gates's frustration at the tortuous nature of decision-making in Obama's National Security Council and attempts at unprecedentedly intrusive controlling by the White House and NSC staff, no word of dissatisfaction was permitted by her to reach the press. There was an absolute ban by her on any negative briefing by the department on other parts of the administration and especially the White House of the kind that from time to time had been current under other Secretaries of State.

---------- CHAPTER 12 ----------

IRAQ: AN APOLOGY

I N THE AUTUMN of 2002, with the Bush administration boasting of iron-clad intelligence about
Saddam Hussein's weapons of mass destruction,
Hillary cast her vote in the Senate in favour of military
action if diplomatic efforts, including the work of the
UN weapons inspectors, failed. In the memoir of her
term as Secretary of State, Hillary makes a comprehensive apology. 'I came to deeply regret giving President
Bush the benefit of the doubt on that vote.'[53] She had
voted in favour, because she believed that Saddam

had weapons of mass destruction and that his was a horrible regime but also, probably, in part at least, to bolster her national security credentials against any future Republican opponent. But the vote was to prove fatal to her by the time of her contest with Obama for the Democratic Party nomination in 2007/8. Given the very narrow margin (150,000 votes) of Obama's victory against her, it seemed at the time that it had cost her the nomination, and the Presidency.

Her unequivocal apology is intended to clear away this toxic baggage from her next campaign, though she will be reminded by the Democratic left that she did not just vote for the war, but continued to support it for many years thereafter. The one thing she voted against, partly, as she acknowledged, for political reasons, was General Petraeus's 'surge', which helped to improve the situation sufficiently for the US to start to withdraw its forces from Iraq. With a sectarian Shiite government, in thrall to the Iranians, in power in Baghdad, there is nothing popular in the US about the Iraq war today. She should, she said, have stated her regret earlier and in the plainest language, but she had cast her 2002 vote in good faith.[54]

Although Iraq remained a continuing concern for the Obama administration, featuring still quite prominently in Bob Gates's memoir, beyond the apology, it scarcely does so in *Hard Choices*, as if this were a subject she never wanted to hear of again. The US ambassador, Christopher Hill, felt that Iraq was a subject in which she was deliberately uninterested.

The offensive by the Syrian and Iraqi jihadists of the Islamic State, the massacres they have perpetrated and the barbaric executions of US hostages in northern Iraq have now forced it back centre stage on the US political agenda, with Hillary supporting air strikes and Obama being fiercely criticised for what has been perceived as being a hesitant and belated response to the threat posed by them.

CHAPTER 13

'BETTER TO BE
CAUGHT TRYING'

HILLARY FROM TIME to time was criticised, mainly outside the US, for not making a full frontal attempt to resolve the Israel/Palestine problem of the kind later attempted, with no success, by John Kerry. With Benjamin Netanyahu installed as Prime Minister of Israel and Hamas in Gaza, the criticism is hard to justify.

Hillary had made many visits to Israel over the past thirty years. She was full of admiration for Yitzhak

Rabin (for whom she rescinded the no-smoking ban in the White House) and his contribution to the Oslo peace accord with Yasser Arafat, leading to their celebrated handshake on the lawn of the White House on 13 September 1993. Two years later, she had been distraught attending Rabin's funeral, following his assassination by an Israeli extremist. Hillary had been an early advocate of Palestinian statehood, before it became US policy. She had been appalled at Arafat's failure to accept Ehud Barak's peace offer in the Camp David discussion in 2000 that would have given the Palestinians statehood, with a capital in east Jerusalem.

As Obama was about to become President in January 2009, the Israelis launched an invasion of Gaza to stop a spate of rocket attacks on Israel. Hillary appointed Senator George Mitchell, veteran of the Northern Ireland peace progress, as her special envoy for Middle East peace. She was an admirer of the Israeli President, Shimon Peres, and of the outgoing Foreign Minister, Tzipi Livni. As for the incoming Israeli Prime Minister, Benjamin ('Bibi') Netanyahu, she had known him for years as a critic of the Oslo accords and sceptical of a two-state solution.

The Obama White House started out by demanding a freeze of the rapidly growing Israeli settlements on the West Bank. Obama's chief of staff, Rahm Emmanuel, himself a former volunteer with the Israeli defence force, believed that unless the administration took a strong position from the outset, the Israelis would simply ignore them. The result was a highly personal standoff between Obama and Netanyahu. Hillary devoted much effort to persuading Netanyahu to agree to a ten-month halt for new settlements on the West Bank, but not in east Jerusalem. Hillary's friend, the Defence Minister, Ehud Barak, was more open to compromise. Mahmoud Abbas, head of the Palestinian Authority, which had succeeded, with US and other help, in raising living standards on the West Bank, denounced the freeze as inadequate, but became very concerned when it was due to expire. In March 2010, while Vice-President Biden was in Tel Aviv, the Israelis announced a plan to build 1,600 new housing units in east Jerusalem. A furious Obama told Netanyahu that this was a personal insult to him and to the United States. Obama broke off a subsequent meeting with Netanyahu in the White House, leaving him to his own devices for an hour.

A month before the settlement freeze was about to expire, Abbas agreed to resume direct negotiations. On 1 September 2010, Obama and Hillary held a meeting at the White House with Netanyahu, Abbas, President Mubarak of Egypt and King Abdullah of Jordan. The talks continued at the State Department and then, two weeks later, at Sharm al-Sheikh on the Red Sea, before moving on to Jerusalem. There the discussions became deadlocked, among other things, on Netanyahu's insistence that Israeli troops must patrol the Jordan–Palestine border for 'decades' after the recognition of a Palestinian state. Netanyahu refused to extend the settlement freeze, causing Abbas to withdraw, with no direct meeting between them since.[55]

Hillary did not give up, holding further meetings with Abbas and Barak at the UN General Assembly, with Obama calling for the moratorium to be extended and her telling Barak that its collapse would be a disaster for Israel and the United States. In November, Netanyahu agreed to a ninety-day moratorium on new settlements on the West Bank only in return for $3 billion of additional military aid. This initiative got nowhere.

Obama made a statement calling for a two-state solution based on the 1967 frontiers with some agreed swaps of territory. Relations between him and Netanyahu remained as dire as ever, with Netanyahu denouncing US attempts to reach a nuclear agreement with Iran. He had been able to defy yet another US President because the only effective sanction, a suspension of financial or military support, would cause a political earthquake in the US, with the administration accused of endangering Israel's security. Hillary was no more prepared to

contemplate that than Obama, or any of his predecessors since Eisenhower had been, particularly given her
lack of confidence in the Palestinian commitment to a
lasting peace. If she were elected President, Hillary, for
sure, would try again, but with no great expectations as
to the chances of success.

✻   ✻   ✻

In November 2012, Hillary was accompanied by the
Defense Secretary, Leon Panetta, on a visit to Australia.
The Israeli Defence Minister, Barak, called Panetta to
say that in response to a rocket bombardment of Israeli
territory by Hamas, the Israelis were about to launch
air strikes on Gaza. Hillary was clear that every country had the right to defend itself and the Israelis were
bound to respond to the hundreds of rockets being fired
at them from Gaza. She called the new Egyptian Foreign
Minister, appointed by the Muslim Brotherhood government, to urge him to talk to Hamas. Obama called
the new Egyptian President, Morsi, and Netanyahu.

The 'Iron Dome' Israeli air defence system the US
had helped to build was proving quite effective against
the rocket attacks, but the Israelis by now had mobilised 75,000 reservists for a ground attack. As Hillary
joined Obama in Thailand, he was very cautious about

her going to the region to launch a mediating effort that might fail or look as if they were undercutting Israel. Hillary insisted that it was 'better to be caught trying'.

On meeting Netanyahu in Tel Aviv, she was told that they had contacted the Egyptians, with no success. The Israelis would give her some time, but not much. She met Mahmoud Abbas, head of the Palestinian Authority, but his influence was limited, upstaged by that of Hamas. On 21 November, she saw President Morsi in Cairo. She was relieved to find that Morsi was prepared to work with her, at any rate to avoid an Israeli invasion of Gaza. At zero hour, the Israelis would cease hostilities and Egypt was to ensure that Hamas stopped rocket and mortar attacks. Obama phoned Netanyahu to promise US assistance in combating weapons-smuggling into Gaza. To Hillary's relief, the ceasefire held better than expected. The Muslim Brotherhood government, in her opinion, 'would never seem as credible again as it did that day'.[56]

CHAPTER 14

THE ARAB SPRING

THE NEXT EPISODE was a far from successful one for US foreign policy. Hillary had known the Egyptian President, Hosni Mubarak, and his wife Suzanne since her days as First Lady. She had said in 2009 that she considered them to be friends of her family. She acknowledged that Mubarak ruled Egypt like a pharaoh, but for three decades he had been a key ally of the US, committed to the peace treaty with Israel and to a two-state solution for Israel and Palestine. When, following the overthrow of the

regime in Tunisia, mass demonstrations broke out in
Tahrir Square in Cairo, Hillary was extremely cautious.
She called for an 'orderly transition' to democracy
and sent the former US ambassador Frank Wisner to
argue with Mubarak for this. But both she and Bob
Gates feared that rapid US abandonment of a long-
standing ally would send a dangerous message to the
Saudis and Gulf rulers. She told the President that if
Mubarak fell 'it may all work out fine in twenty-five
years', but the road was likely to be decidedly rocky
between now and then.[57]

Obama and the White House staff had no such inhi-
bitions. They wanted to be on the right side of history,
at any rate as interpreted by CNN. Obama announced
that he had told Mubarak that the transition 'must
begin now'. This immediately was publicised, with the
White House press secretary adding that 'now began
yesterday'.

Mubarak resigned on 11 February. Visiting Tahrir
Square in March, Hillary found the crowd to be completely disorganised, leaving her fearing that they would
end up handing the country to the Muslim Brotherhood
or the military by default. Mubarak's Foreign Minister
had warned her of an Islamist takeover: his daughters
did not want to end up wearing the niqab, as in Saudi
Arabia.[58]

When the elections were narrowly won by Moham-
med Morsi and the Muslim Brotherhood, despite their
having promised not to propose a candidate for President, western governments attempted for a while to
convince themselves that, despite Morsi's close ties
to Hamas and their published views on theocracy and
Israel, the Brotherhood were relative moderates deserv-
ing of support. The Saudis derided this, asking Hillary
if the US really wanted to see a Sunni version of Iran
established in Egypt. Morsi dismissed the head of the
armed forces, declared that his decisions could not
be reviewed by the courts and established the principle of *sharia* law. In 2013, he was overthrown by the
Egyptian military and replaced by General al-Sisi in
a crackdown supported by the Saudis and the Gulf
rulers. So much for this episode of the Arab Spring.

✳   ✳   ✳

In her memoir, Hillary wrestles with the fact that, despite
American and her own attachment to human rights, the
United States' key allies in the Arab world were and are
highly conservative traditional monarchies with a commitment to reform, if at all, only at a snail's pace. In view
of the events in Egypt and Tunisia, she felt that Middle
East leaders were sitting on a powder keg. In a speech

in Qatar on 13 February 2011, she said that people had
grown tired of corrupt institutions and a stagnant political order. The region's foundations were sinking into the
sand. Those who clung to the status quo would encourage extremist elements preying on desperation and
poverty.[59] The accompanying journalists were impressed
by how blunt she had been. Her aides raved about the
speech, which they described as inspirational. Just how
inspiring it would turn out to be, she was about to
find out.

The US and her dilemma was posed in a particularly
difficult form by demonstrations by elements of the Shia
majority in Bahrain, home base for the US navy in the
Gulf, against the Emir and the Sunni ruling class. On 17
February 2012, a number of protesters were killed by
the police. She told the Foreign Minister that this was a
recipe for more trouble and sent a key aide, Jeff Feltman,
to Bahrain to try to mediate between the government and
the protest leaders. She was well aware, however, that the
Emir, the Saudis and the other Gulf rulers regarded
the protests as having been orchestrated by Iran. On 14
March, thousands of Saudi troops entered Bahrain with
650 armoured vehicles. Five hundred police followed
from the United Arab Emirates. The US, deliberately,
was given no forewarning of their intention to intervene. In a BBC interview, Hillary had to admit that

the US had very little leverage with its allies on an issue of this kind.[60]

CHAPTER 15

FIASCO IN SYRIA

THE INSURRECTION AGAINST the Assad regime in Syria began in 2011. Despite pressure from the Arab League, the Russians and Chinese vetoed UN sanctions against Assad, who intensified the repression, with tanks and aircraft attacking residential areas. Assad was getting military support from Iran and Hezbollah. The Saudi and some other Arab governments started arming the Sunni rebels. Kofi Annan's attempts to get support for a transitional government came to nothing. Hillary began canvassing the idea of the US giving arms to and training 'moderate' rebels. General Petraeus put forward a plan to do so.

But Obama did not want to get involved in another sectarian war in the Middle East. Hillary got a fair hearing, but he did not agree. The administration agreed to increase humanitarian relief supplies but, as Hillary observed, these were no more than Band-Aids.[61]

By March 2013, shortly after she left office, evidence started accumulating that the regime had begun using chemical weapons, of which they were known to have large stockpiles. In August 2012, Obama had declared that using chemical weapons was a red line for the United States, taken as indicating that if the Syrian regime crossed that line, there would be a military response. In June 2013 the White House confirmed that it believed that chemical weapons had been used on a small scale on multiple occasions.

In August 2013 the regime launched a massive chemical weapons attack on rebel-held areas of Damascus, killing around 1,400 people. Obama said that the US could 'not accept a world where women and children and innocent civilians are gassed on a terrible scale … If we fail to act, the Assad regime will see no reason to stop using chemical weapons.'

Plans for the obvious retaliation, a missile or air strike on the Republican Guard base from which the missiles

containing gas had been launched, were thrown into disarray when the British Prime Minister, David Cameron,
lost a vote in the House of Commons to authorise the
use of force in Syria. Two days later, Obama announced
his intention to order air strikes to deter and degrade the
future use of chemical weapons by the Assad regime. But
in a move that 'surprised many' (and appalled Hillary
and the Defense Secretary, Leon Panetta), Obama said
that he would seek authorisation from Congress, which
was then in recess. Hillary watched the failure to uphold
a crucial international norm with consternation. She
worked with her successor, John Kerry, and the Republican senator Bob Corker to try to get a vote in favour
of action. Kerry's throwaway remark that Assad could
avoid it by handing over his chemical weapons was
seized on by the Russians to protect their ally.

Hillary told Obama that it was the threat of force
that had caused the Russians to act. If he was not confident of winning a vote in Congress, he should get
the Russians to help dismantle Assad's chemical weapons arsenal, with the involvement of UN inspectors.[62]
Obama regarded this as a great victory for diplomacy.
Hillary was more concerned at the spectacle of a US
President drawing a red line and allowing it to be
crossed. While the Syrians have handed over a massive
amount of chemical weapons, which they always denied

possessing, they have continued to use mustard gas and chlorine against the rebels, while the insurrection itself has been largely taken over, first by Al Qaeda and then by the other ultra-radical Islamic extremist movement, the Islamic State.

Hillary since has argued that the failure to supply weapons to the moderate opponents of the Syrian regime contributed to the takeover of the resistance by the jihadists, getting her into a public argument with Obama for the first time since serving as his Secretary of State.

CHAPTER 16

WRESTLING WITH IRAN

A S A SENATOR, Hillary was a staunch supporter of sanctions against Iran, declaring that
the US 'could not, should not and must not'
permit Iran to build nuclear weapons. In April 2008
she declared that if Iran used nuclear weapons against
Israel, it would be 'obliterated'.[63]

On becoming President, Obama sent two private messages to Ayatollah Khamenei and recorded
video messages for the Iranian people, with no response.
In June 2009, the opposition Green movement in Iran

was crushed by the regime. In September, the Iranians were obliged to admit the existence of a hitherto secret uranium enrichment facility near Qom. Obama and Hillary presented the evidence about it to Medvedev and Lavrov. Medvedev told the press that in some cases 'sanctions are inevitable', but the Chinese were reluctant. Hillary became exasperated at attempts by Brazil and Turkey to broker an agreement that would impose no real constraints on Iran. In meetings with the Chinese President and Premier in Beijing, Hillary emphasised that the issue was critical for the US and managed to get their support for a UN Security Council resolution in June 2010 imposing tougher sanctions on Iran.

In Washington she held a meeting with Senator Chris Dodd and Congressman Howard Berman, both of them, like her, staunch supporters of Israel, about their respective versions of sanctions against Iran, which they were sponsoring in the Senate and the House. The aim was to punish foreign entities if, ignoring US sanctions, they did business with the regime.

Hillary wanted a version that would give foreign companies incentives to get out of Iran, enabling them to avoid sanctions if they could show that they were on an exit path. As a senator, she had accused the Bush administration of not doing enough about Iran. Now she was trying to moderate the Congressional bills.

The administration had been telling the Russians and Chinese that if they put pressure on the Iranians to abandon their military nuclear programme, their companies would not suffer from sanctions against them. The American Israel Public Affairs Committee (AIPAC), typically the most powerful lobbying organisation vis-à-vis Congress, was demanding stronger action. Hillary and her deputy, Jim Steinberg, felt strongly that they must get international cooperation, not just unilateral US action, to put effective pressure on Iran. Hillary was successful in getting the 'closely cooperating country exemption' added to the bill.[64]

In 2011, the Sultan of Oman offered to arrange direct talks between the Americans and Iranians. The first encounter took place at official level in July 2012. The European Union, meanwhile, had been persuaded to ban the import of Iranian oil.

In previous instances, for example the crackdown on Solidarity in Poland, the US had been unsuccessful in getting effective support for sanctions from its allies. In the case of Iran, however (and of North Korea and Sudan), not Hillary, but the US Treasury and Justice Department had worked out ways of making the sanctions stick and really hurt. Multi-national corporations and banks were warned that if they circumvented US sanctions, they would face massive fines (which have since been imposed) and the potential seizure of their assets in the US.

These measures and the regime's own mismanagement inflicted serious economic damage on Iran. In the June 2013 election, the former Iranian negotiator and relative moderate Hassan Rouhani was elected President. At the end of the year, an interim agreement was reached with Iran entailing substantial sanctions relief in return for inspections and an attempt to freeze the Iranian nuclear programme which, however, still is being resisted by those who really hold the levers of power in Iran.

CHAPTER 17

SAVING THE PLANET

I N DECEMBER 2009, the United Nations Frame-
work Convention on Climate Change convened in
Copenhagen in an attempt to bridge the wide gap
between developed and developing countries in their
efforts to combat climate change. The US Senate had
refused to ratify the Kyoto accord and also had blocked
Obama's attempts to introduce 'cap and trade' legislation
to limit carbon emissions. Meanwhile, however, the US
was reducing those emissions faster than other countries as
a result of a massive shift in energy usage from coal to gas.

Visiting India earlier in the year, Hillary had been told publicly by the Environment Minister that addressing climate change was the responsibility of wealthy countries like the US and not of the developing world. On the other side of the argument were the Europeans, still hoping to extend the Kyoto accord that, in Hillary's view, had placed big burdens on themselves while giving countries like China and India a free pass.[65]

In an effort to break the deadlock, Hillary made the extraordinary announcement, contributed to by Gordon Brown, that the US was prepared to lead an effort by developed countries to mobilise $100 billion *annually* by 2020 from public and private sources to help the poorest nations, if they could reach agreement on limiting emissions. It was not clear how these funds would be mobilised and the announcement appeared to have little effect.

The conference was very poorly prepared and chaotic. At the end of a long and intensely frustrating session, Hillary found herself in the early hours standing on the pavement with Sarkozy, waiting interminably for their cars. 'I want to die,' said Sarkozy, rolling his eyes to the sky. Given how stuck the talks were, the White House were questioning whether Obama should join her in Copenhagen, but Hillary urged him to come.

The Chinese had been avoiding them and, instead,

Premier Wen Jiabao had called a 'secret' meeting with the Indians, Brazilians and South Africans to concert their positions. Learning about the meeting, Obama and Hillary decided to gatecrash it, despite an effort by Chinese officials physically to prevent them entering the room. In the meeting, the Chinese resisted any robust reporting and verification requirements, but Manmohan Singh for India and Jacob Zuma for South Africa were more conciliatory. In the end they all agreed, with Wen Jiabao over-ruling a member of his delegation, that for the first time, all the major economies would make national commitments to reduce carbon emissions by 2020 and would report on this.

Next, they had to deal with the Europeans, who had imposed draconian legal limits on their own emissions and wanted everyone else to do the same, which Congress, let alone the Chinese, would not accept.

Hillary followed this up with the Climate and Clean Air Coalition programme in February 2012, concentrating on the reduction of the 'super-pollutants', including methane, black carbon and hydrofluorocarbons (HFCs). With the Norwegian Foreign Minister, she made the mandatory trip to witness shrinking glaciers, as she did with Senator John McCain and two other Republican senators in Alaska. She worried that the opening up of waterways in the Arctic could lead to damaging mineral exploitation and facilitate potential militarisation of the Arctic by Russia.

Hillary, therefore, has no time for climate change deniers. But she is an economic realist, who has no intention of rendering the US uncompetitive in attempting to deal with the problem. The Chinese have begun making greater efforts to do so for their own reasons. As a result of technological innovation, Hillary has noted with satisfaction, US energy input prices have fallen to roughly half the level of those in Europe.[66]

CHAPTER 18

OLD FRIENDS

HILLARY DEVOTES JUST twenty-two of the 632 pages of *Hard Choices* to Europe. She is unfailingly polite and positive about her European counterparts, especially the British. David Miliband flattered her effusively by telling her that her predecessors had left her a lot of problems, but he thought she was the right Hercules for this task. She found him 'smart, creative and attractive, with a ready smile'. She felt that the dogged and intelligent, but embattled Gordon Brown had been 'dealt a bad hand', neglecting the role he had played in dealing it himself. David Cameron was 'intellectually curious'. He and Obama enjoyed each other's company. She approved of William Hague's biography of Wilberforce. At a farewell dinner he hosted for her at the British embassy in Washington, he showed himself to be 'the David Beckham of toasting!' Cathy Ashton turned out to be refreshingly down to earth for a baroness.

It is easy to make fun of these anodyne observations but, without a doubt, Hillary is an anglophile.

Her main political love affair, however, was with Tony and Cherie Blair. To Hillary, New Labour and the New Democrats seemed to be about exactly the same things. She could not see any policy differences between them. She supported Blair when her husband was wavering over Kosovo. She would have been less than human not to be disappointed when Blair developed such a cosy relationship with George W. Bush, but remains on friendly terms with the Blairs.

Hillary was extremely proud of the role her husband played in supporting the Northern Ireland peace process. Her final overseas visit as Secretary of State was to Northern Ireland in December 2012. She recalled visiting Northern Ireland with her husband in 1995, the first ever visit there by a US President, and the reception they got when they switched on the Christmas tree lights in Belfast. She had returned to Northern Ireland nearly every year to the end of the decade and as a senator continued to show support for the peace process. With Melanne Verveer she had set up an international women's organisation called Vital Voices. In 1998 she organised a conference of the organisation in Belfast to support the women's groups campaigning for peace. The Good Friday Agreement, signed that year, she regarded as a triumph of diplomacy, 'especially for Bill and Senator George Mitchell', forgetting the role of the British and Irish governments.

As the British ambassador in the US at the time, I was furious when Bill Clinton gave a visa to Gerry Adams in the absence of any undertaking by him to dissociate himself from terrorism. But I was confident that, thereafter, he would come under intense US pressure to do so and that the US could play an important supportive role, provided they undertook never to interfere in the Major and, subsequently, Blair governments' negotiations with the parties, an undertaking I asked them to give and which they observed scrupulously.

As Secretary of State, Hillary continued in this vein. On a visit in October 2009 and in frequent phone calls to the Northern Ireland First Minister, Peter Robinson, and the deputy First Minister, Martin McGuinness, she urged them to overcome their differences about policing

and the administration of justice and to disarm the para-
military groups. She was thrilled that the Queen, visiting
Belfast in June 2012, showed herself prepared to shake
McGuinness's hand.

*   *   *

Among the other Europeans, her favourite counterparts
were the French. She admired the French Foreign Minister Bernard Kouchner for having founded *Médecins Sans
Frontières*. She worked well with his successor, Alain
Juppé, and, subsequently, with President Hollande's
Foreign Minister, Laurent Fabius. But her particular
enthusiasm was reserved for Nicolas Sarkozy, who she
describes as always dramatic – and fun. She found it
hard to get a word in edgeways, but 'never tired of trying'. She admired his determination that France should
continue to play a leading role in world affairs, as over
Libya. On one visit to Paris, climbing the steps of the
Elysée, she lost a shoe in front of the attendant pho-
tographers. He seized her hand and helped her regain
it. She sent him a copy of the photograph inscribed, 'I
may not be Cinderella but you'll always be my Prince
Charming.'

The more powerful leader, however, very obviously
was Angela Merkel, who Hillary found to be decisive,

astute and straightforward. She was delighted to be presented by Merkel with a German newspaper photograph of the two of them standing side by side, hands clasped in front of their trouser suits, with the heads cropped out. The readers were invited to judge which was Merkel and which was Hillary.

Hillary did have worries, however, about Merkel's European policies. She wanted Germany to help re-flate the weaker eurozone economies, rather than imposing too much austerity on them. Angela Merkel was having none of this, unsurprisingly since, as Hillary herself acknowledged, she was 'carrying Europe on her shoulders'.[67]

* * *

Few of the other European leaders rate a mention in her memoir, except for Erdoğan in Turkey, about whom she has mixed feelings, but she does include a tribute to NATO's success in incorporating the countries of eastern Europe and continued relevance in the context, for instance, of the Russian annexation of Crimea. NATO took the lead in the 2011 intervention in Libya, in which the US provided special military capabilities but, she noted with satisfaction, the European allies flew 75 per cent of the sorties and were responsible for destroying most of the targets attacked in Libya. A decade before, the US had flown 90 per cent of the sorties in Kosovo.

CHAPTER 19

VICTORY IN LIBYA

IN FEBRUARY 2011, the North African demonstrations spread to Libya, only to encounter fierce repression by Gaddafi. Gaddafi had few friends in the Arab world: Libya was suspended from the Arab League. On 26 February, the UN Security Council imposed an arms embargo and measures against Gaddafi, his family and senior officials. There was talk of a 'no-fly zone' to prevent him using his aircraft against the rebels.

This caused a split right down the middle of the Obama foreign policy team, with Biden, McDonough,

Gates and the military opposed to getting involved. The
UN ambassador, Susan Rice, and Samantha Power on
the NSC staff were insisting that the US must step in
to prevent a massacre.

Hillary, initially, had been cautious. The US still was
bogged down in wars in Iraq and Afghanistan. Nor
was it clear what the opposition forces amounted to in
Libya. Nicolas Sarkozy from the outset had been the
strongest advocate of intervention. He wanted France
to be seen to be playing a leading role in world affairs.
But Gates could not see what vital interest the US had
at stake in Libya and came close to threatening to resign
over the US intervening there. In meetings he would
ask: 'Can I just finish the two wars we're in before you
go looking for new ones?' The Pentagon were warning
that imposition of a no-fly zone on its own would not
suffice to halt the advance of Gaddafi's tanks.

On 10 March Hillary told Congress that 'absent
international authorisation, the United States acting
alone would be stepping into a situation whose consequences are unforeseeable. And I know that's the
way our military feels.' She felt that, too often, other
countries urged the US to intervene without being prepared to make much of a contribution themselves.[68]
Her friend the former NATO commander General
Wesley Clark warned against another US commitment

to regime change: 'Libya's politics hardly foreshadow a clear outcome.'

Arriving in Paris for a meeting on Libya, Hillary was surprised to be told by the United Arab Emirates Foreign Minister that they would themselves be prepared to participate in an air offensive against Gaddafi. She also got a fierce lecture from him about US criticism of the regime in Bahrain. As well as Sarkozy, the British Foreign Secretary, William Hague, also was pressing for action. For Hillary, 'that counted for a lot', as she felt that Hague would be wary of adopting such a position without having thought it through.

On 14 March in Paris, she met one of the Libyan opposition leaders, Mahmoud Jibril, a meeting facilitated by the French polemicist Bernard-Henri Lévy, who, to Hillary's amusement, lived up to his reputation of appearing with his shirt unbuttoned to the navel. Jibril, a political scientist from the University of Pittsburgh, represented the moderate face of the Libyan resistance. As Hillary observed, the US had learned the hard way in Iraq that overthrowing a dictator was one thing, organising a credible and competent alternative government quite another.[69]

But Gaddafi's troops by now were closing in on Benghazi, with the prospect of a humanitarian catastrophe. When Sarkozy told her that he was about to ring Obama to insist on action to prevent a massacre, Hillary, knowing how wary Obama would be, told Sarkozy not to let him off the line until he had an answer!

On 15 March Hillary flew to Cairo to insist that the Arab League must take the lead in calling for military action, which they did. The UAE, Qatar and, subsequently, Jordan undertook to participate in the military campaign. Two days later Gaddafi on television told the inhabitants of Benghazi that 'we are coming tonight and there will be no mercy'.

In the National Security Council meeting on 17 March Biden, Gates, Mullen for the US military, the national security advisor (Donilon) and the deputy national security advisor (McDonough) all remained opposed. Obama described it as a 51–49 call. It was as well that he made it as he did as, otherwise, the US would have been seen as failing to support its key allies in Europe and the region and would have been held responsible for the ensuing slaughter in Benghazi. He agreed that the US should seek to press through a UN Security Council resolution authorising 'all necessary measures' to protect civilians. But he and Gates insisted that most of the sorties would have to be flown by the allies and there would be no US boots on the ground.[70] After the initial bombardment the US would be 'leading from behind'.

Hillary called Lavrov. Russia had been strongly against a no-fly zone but Hillary assured him that there would be no US troops on the ground and the Russians had no interest in propping up Gaddafi. Lavrov said they would abstain. He subsequently complained that Hillary had sold him a humanitarian operation, not regime change, but he must have known where things were heading. The Chinese also abstained, as did Brazil, India and, to Hillary's disappointment, Germany.

Sarkozy convened another meeting in Paris on 19 March. Just before the meeting began, Sarkozy told Hillary and David Cameron that French aircraft already were on their way to Libya. The Americans were not amused since, as Hillary put it, they had unique capabilities and it had to fall to them to destroy the Libyan air defence system.[71] This they did by firing more than a hundred cruise missiles from US warships in the Mediterranean, targeting also Gaddafi's forces advancing on Benghazi.

It was now largely over to the allies, but their efforts had to be coordinated. There was the usual wrangle with the French about this being done by NATO, which in the end they accepted, once Hillary agreed with the Foreign Minister, Alain Juppé, that there could be a political committee to give 'policy guidance'.

The military campaign lasted longer than expected,

but by August 2011 the rebels had captured Tripoli.
Hillary arrived there in October, to find herself being
greeted by militia fighters chanting 'God is great, USA!'
She was, she said, proud to stand on the soil of a free
Libya. Jibril by now was interim Prime Minister, at
the head of a precarious coalition of disparate opposition factions. She called for Gaddafi to be 'captured or
killed soon'.[72] Two days later, Gaddafi was killed, with
Hillary shedding no tears for him.

CHAPTER 20

DISASTER IN BENGHAZI

FOLLOWING THE REVOLT against Gaddafi, the career foreign service officer Chris Stevens, an experienced Arabist who had served in Libya before, was based in Benghazi, liaising with the rebel leaders, from April until November 2011. In May 2012 he was asked by Hillary to return to Tripoli as the US ambassador. In March his predecessor had asked unsuccessfully for a delay in the drawdown of security at the embassy in a still unstable environment. Stevens also asked the State Department's security department for delay after a bomb blew a hole in the wall of the Benghazi compound. The request was denied.

Conditions were most threatening in Benghazi, so much so that the British closed their consulate there. Some additional work was done on the US compound in Benghazi before Stevens arrived on a visit there in September 2012 to judge whether he could recommend the establishment of a permanent consulate. He reported to Washington that in response to US support for Jibril to become Prime Minister, local militia members were threatening to stop protecting Americans. Meanwhile, the embassy in Cairo had been attacked by protesters demonstrating against an anti-Muslim video produced in the US.

On the evening of 11 September, around sixty armed militia stormed the US compound in Benghazi. Stevens was trapped inside with one colleague and five security officers. The house in which they took refuge was set on fire with diesel fuel. A US security guard tried to lead Stevens and his colleague Stan Smith through the dense smoke to an escape hatch, but lost them along the way and was unable to fight his way back through the fumes. The security officers survived, but Stevens and Smith were unable to escape from the building.[73]

Hillary had called the Libyan President, Magariaf, to ask for help. At 3 a.m. the Libyan Prime Minister confirmed that Stevens had been killed. The much better-protected CIA safe house in Benghazi, which had been visited by Stevens, also was attacked, with two CIA officers killed by mortar fire.

On the next morning, Hillary stood next to the President as he reported the disaster. She then rushed back to the State Department to greet Obama, who delivered a spontaneous and moving address in praise of the foreign service.

The White House wanted Hillary to appear on the Sunday television shows, which she declined to do. The UN ambassador, Susan Rice, was asked to do so instead. Hillary and Obama went to Andrews air force base to meet the military plane carrying the bodies of the four dead Americans and meet their families. Hillary said: 'We will wipe away our tears, stiffen our spines and face the future undaunted.' The people of Libya and Egypt, she added, 'did not trade the tyranny of a dictator for the tyranny of a mob'.[74]

Meanwhile, the CIA had been asked to prepare talking points for Rice and others to use. A first draft suggested that the attack in Benghazi had been triggered by the demonstrations in Cairo. The CIA also included a reference, raised by the State Department, to warnings by them about the threat of Al Qaeda-linked terrorism in Libya. But the talking points for Rice were pared to a minimum by the NSC staff. Rice told *Meet the Press* that what happened in Benghazi appeared to be a 'spontaneous reaction' to what had happened in Cairo and that 'opportunist extremist elements came to the consulate as this was unfolding'.

Susan Rice stuck closely to the abbreviated speaking note she had been given, but soon found that she had been left hopelessly exposed. In fact, there had been no demonstration in Benghazi.

Hillary's meeting with senators on 20 September went very badly. Senator Lindsey Graham accused the administration team of dissembling. Senator Susan Collins asked how all five members of the protection team had got away unharmed. Hillary appeared to be acknowledging that it had been a terrorist attack, thereby disavowing Susan Rice. The episode ended Rice's hopes of succeeding Hillary as Secretary of State and Hillary's of being able to regard freeing Libya from Gaddafi as a major achievement. She also knew that Benghazi would be raised mercilessly by her Republican opponents to try to block her path to the White House.

The Republicans sought to exploit the Benghazi attack in the 2012 presidential election campaign with an advertisement that read: 'Security Requests Denied. Four Americans Dead. And an Administration Whose Story Is Still Changing.' Hillary declared that, as Secretary of State, she accepted responsibility.

Hillary appointed an Accountability Review Board, led by the former chairman of the joint chiefs of staff Admiral Mullen and retired ambassador Thomas Pickering, to review the security failings in Benghazi. Their report was highly critical of the State Department officials responsible for diplomatic security.

On 23 January 2013 the still convalescent Hillary, wearing dark glasses, attended a Senate hearing on Benghazi. She defended Susan Rice as having had no intention to mislead anyone. She had used the material she had been given. In exasperation she said, 'What difference at this point does it make' (what triggered the attack)? The Republican senator Rand Paul, who had national political ambitions, said that, 'with your leaving, you accept culpability for the worst tragedy since 9/11'. For failing to read the cables from Benghazi about security, he argued, she should have been relieved of her post. Her erstwhile friend the Republican senator Lindsey Graham claimed on television that Hillary had 'got away with murder'.

Susan Rice was obliged to withdraw from consideration as Obama's nominee to succeed Hillary, with the mantle falling instead on the veteran Democratic senator John Kerry.

Benghazi continued to haunt Hillary. In January 2014 the US Senate intelligence committee, chaired by the Democratic senator Dianne Feinstein, published its report on the Benghazi attacks. It said that the intelligence community had produced hundreds of reports in the preceding months warning that militias and terrorist groups had the capability and intent to attack US and other western targets in Libya, citing several of these reports. There had been over twenty security incidents in Benghazi including, on 11 June 2012, an attack on the convoy of the British ambassador. Ambassador Stevens and other US officials in Libya had made several requests for more security, with hardly any response from the State Department. Ambassador Stevens had himself declined two offers of a security team from the US military.

The committee noted the CIA's belief that the attacks had not involved a lot of pre-planning. It accepted the possibility that the attacks had not been decided until the day on which they took place. There had been no protests at the mission prior to the attacks. The Libyan authorities had proved incapable of responding to the attacks and, since then, had not shown the will to take action against those responsible. The talking points provided to Susan Rice had been inaccurate.

The Democratic majority on the committee concluded that the attacks were 'likely preventable', given the warnings about the deteriorating security situation.

The Republicans on the committee, including Senator Marco Rubio, criticised the testimony of Pat Kennedy, the under-secretary responsible for management, as 'particularly specious'. No State Department official had been disciplined for their failure to take action in response to the requests from US personnel in Libya. Mr Kennedy should have used better judgement and should be held accountable. The initial talking points had been edited to limit the damage to the administration, with General Petraeus acknowledging that this was the NSC staff's call. The deputy assistant secretary, Charlene Lamb, had refused to explain her actions to the committee, yet had been reinstated by the State Department. She had rejected several requests from the regional security officers. 'Unfortunately, however, the final responsibility for security at diplomatic facilities lies with the former Secretary of State, Hillary Clinton.' Her failure to take action clearly made a difference in the case of the four murdered Americans.[75]

In *Hard Choices* Hillary indignantly dismisses the notion that the security officers and the team at the CIA compound did not do everything they could to save the ambassador. She lists the many other cases in which US diplomats had been killed on duty. She did not see the requests from Tripoli for more security. Apart from the independent Accountability Review Board, the incident had been investigated by eight Congressional committees. As Secretary of State, she accepted responsibility for what had occurred, but was not clear what more she could have done about it.[76]

Most people, probably, would agree with her, but not her political opponents. The Republicans in the House of Representatives have launched yet another inquiry into what happened in Benghazi, as a stick to beat her with every inch of the way through a possible presidential campaign. To the fury of the Americans, the Libyan authorities showed no interest in arresting the head of the radical Islamist group which the US intelligence services concluded had been responsible for the attack so, in 2014, US special forces seized him themselves for questioning and, potentially, trial in the US.

Both Hillary and Gates had turned out to be right about Libya. Hillary surely was right in supporting intervention to prevent a massacre in Benghazi, Gates in foreseeing that the outcome would be entirely unpredictable thereafter. The murder of Chris Stevens was a harbinger of the state of anarchy in which Libya finds itself today.

CHAPTER 21

'AFRICA DOESN'T NEED STRONGMEN. IT NEEDS STRONG INSTITUTIONS.'

A T A TIME when Hillary had never been to Africa, she learned that the anti-apartheid campaigner Helen Suzman was staying at the British embassy in Washington. Helen Suzman was summoned to the White House, with Hillary showing a close interest in the progress towards the 1994 first full democratic election.

After that election, Hillary was thrilled to be

despatched, along with Vice-President Al Gore, to attend Nelson Mandela's inauguration as President. At lunch, Mandela greeted the delegates from around the world, but said that equally important people present were three men who had been his jailers on Robben Island. They had treated him with dignity and respect. He asked them to stand up while he praised them, making a lasting impression on Hillary.

In 1997, she visited South Africa again, this time with Chelsea. Mandela took them with him to visit Robben Island, talking about the choice he had needed to make for reconciliation and against bitterness. Characteristically, he made a particular fuss of Chelsea, asking thereafter to speak to her when telephoned by her parents.

In the course of this visit, she encountered Robert Mugabe, who she found very disconcerting. 'I left believing that he was dangerously unstable and hoping that he would relinquish power.'[77]

In August 2009, visiting South Africa as Secretary of State, she again met Mandela, by now very frail. Hillary had formed a friendship with his wife, Graça Machel, but she found that South Africa 'could be a frustrating partner'. Thabo Mbeki's denialism of the scientific evidence of HIV/AIDS was a tragic mistake and she found the Zuma government also opposing humanitarian interventions even when they were badly needed, as in Libya and the Ivory Coast.

In August 2012, she led a delegation of business leaders from Federal Express, Chevron, Boeing, General Electric and other companies on a visit to South Africa, only for her plane to be held up at the airport in Malawi while she waited for the South African authorities to clear the arrangements for her security team. A jazz evening during that visit led to more dancing and she visited Mandela at his village, Qunu, in the Transkei.

The member of the South African government she admired most and tried to help was Dr Aaron Motsoaledi, the new Minister of Health appointed by President Zuma in May 2009, who had reversed the Mbeki government's neglect of the campaign against AIDS. Hillary met him in South Africa in August that year and worked with him and the Gates Foundation to help South Africa complete the switch to less costly generic drugs, contributing $120 million to help this process along.

In December 2013 Hillary, together with the President and Michelle Obama, George and Laura Bush, Bill and Chelsea, attended Mandela's funeral event in Soweto. They saw Graça Machel again and, on returning to their hotel, Hillary found herself playing a few bars on the piano with Bono.[78]

✳   ✳   ✳

Hillary belongs firmly in the camp of those western leaders who are determined to try to help Africa to develop its potential. But there also are undertones of exasperation at times on the part of this very can-do person about the difficulties she encountered in her efforts to do so.

Will Africa's future, she enquires in *Hard Choices*, be defined more by guns and graft or by growth and better governance? President Obama declared in a speech they crafted together to the parliament in Ghana: 'Africa doesn't need strongmen. It needs strong institutions.'

On a visit to Zambia in 2011 she was asked by a journalist whether the Chinese system did not offer a better model for Africa, as opposed to the notion of good governance, which, he suggested, was largely seen in Africa as 'being imposed by the west'. Hillary applauded China's success in lifting vast numbers of people out of poverty in China, but did not applaud what she saw as their complete disregard of human rights abuses by governments with which they were seeking to do business. It was not western nations who should be concerned most about human rights in Africa, but Africans themselves.

In June 2011, visiting the headquarters of the African

Union in Addis Ababa, she declared that 'the old ways of governing are no longer acceptable, it is time for leaders to lead with accountability, treat their people with dignity, respect their rights and deliver economic opportunity'. Otherwise, it was time for them to go. She noted with regret that during her time as Secretary of State there were coups in Guinea-Bissau, the Central African Republic, the Ivory Coast, Mali and Madagascar.[79]

In Senegal, she played a role in helping to persuade the 85-year-old President Abdoulaye Wade to accept defeat in the 2012 elections. In Liberia, she formed a friendship with the US-educated President, Ellen Johnson Sirleaf, elected after periods of exile and an especially bloody civil war.

She considered corruption to be the major impediment to growth in most of Africa. In August 2009 she met in Nairobi the Nobel Prize winner Wangari Maathai, who had denounced China as 'willing to do business without conditions like respect for human rights' and who impressed her by saying that Africa was not a poor continent. It was rich in resources. Africans needed to demand good governance and accountability from their leaders and from those investing there.

Hillary told the Kenyan President, Mwai Kibaki, and Prime Minister Odinga that the US was concerned about the flawed 2007 election, political violence and rampant corruption. She offered Kenyan and other audiences the example of Botswana, where the government, instead of squandering the revenue from natural resources, had set up a national trust fund that invested the diamond revenues in education and infrastructure, thereby largely dispensing with the need for external aid.

In 2009 Senator Barbara Boxer had been holding hearings of the Senate foreign relations committee about violence against women in war zones, focused on the Democratic Republic of the Congo, where it appeared that the eastern city of Goma had become the rape capital of the world. In August, Hillary descended on Kinshasa. In one of her usual town hall meetings, she found an air of sullen resignation among those she met.

They had, in her opinion, reason to feel hopeless. The government was feckless and incompetent, the roads, schools and hospitals in a terrible state. It was hot and stuffy in the meeting hall and she was asked a question translated as 'What does Mr Clinton think through the mouth of Mrs Clinton?' causing her to snap: 'My husband is not the Secretary of State, I am.' The questioner apologised, saying that he had meant to ask about Obama, and Hillary was sorry that she had snapped at him, even though the remark did her no harm at all.

She flew on to Goma and Lake Kivu. She met President Kabila, by whom she was not impressed. He seemed distracted and unfocused. There followed a visit to the Mugunga refugee camp where Hillary, a great believer in self-help as well as aid, was horrified to find that there was no school, though the camp had been open for a year, and no patrols to help protect the women in it.[80]

Another preoccupation was the conflict in Sudan, where genocide in Darfur and fighting between the Arab north and Christian south had claimed more than two million lives. Eventually an agreement was reached that led to South Sudan becoming an independent state in July 2011.

This, however, was followed immediately by conflict over South Sudan's oil production, which the northern Sudanese would only allow them to export at exorbitant cost. So Hillary flew to Juba in August 2012 to try to broker an agreement. Finding the President of South Sudan resisting, she produced an op-ed piece in the *New York Times* by his former comrade in arms, now a bishop, Elias Taban, urging the need for compromise. A hard-fought bargain was achieved, but Hillary departed with justified worries about the stability of Africa's newest nation state.

The most serious headache of all was Somalia, with the emergence of Al Shabaab, with close ties to Al Qaeda, as a threat to the entire region and piracy posing a serious threat to shipping. In 2009 Hillary helped to get some financial and weapons support to the Somali troops fighting the militants. In August in Nairobi she pledged support for the President of Somalia's interim government, the moderate Islamist Sheikh Sharif.

The Pentagon started training thousands of Somali troops in Uganda, increasing financial support and weapons supplies. In 2012 the Somali factions agreed on elections that led to the formation of a new government. Visiting a US training camp in Uganda, Hillary was intrigued to be shown a new US surveillance drone that looked like a model aircraft, but with sophisticated camera equipment that could be used to track rebel forces. She wanted this technology also to be used to track down the leaders of the Lord's Resistance Army, which had been carrying out atrocities in various parts of central Africa. In 2013, after she had left office, the danger posed by Al Shabaab was further demonstrated when they attacked a shopping mall in Nairobi, killing seventy people.

CHAPTER 22

ONE MILLION AIR MILES

HILLARY PRIDED HERSELF on having travelled nearly one million air miles as Secretary of State and on having visited 112 countries, causing her critics to accuse her of believing in perpetual motion at the expense of more selective intervention. It certainly will be quite a while before another US Secretary of State bothers to stop over in Timor Leste.

This quantitative approach to diplomacy also was thought to have been displayed in her insistence that the State Department should emulate the Pentagon in producing a comprehensive four-year plan setting out its objectives. She had been impressed by an article in *Foreign Affairs* by Anne-Marie Slaughter, arguing that America would benefit more than others from the new 'networked' world of instant and virtually unstoppable world-wide communications. She was appointed as Hillary's director of policy planning and put in charge of the 'top to bottom' Quadrennial Review of the State Department and USAID. After a huge bureaucratic exercise, it was not entirely clear what had been achieved.

Exhausted by four years of intense effort and incessant travel, Hillary was, she said, looking forward to a future of 'beaches and speeches'. In December 2012, following a further killing travel schedule, she fell in her bathroom, hitting her head. She did not see a doctor for a few days, only to find, when she did, that she had suffered a concussion. It was in fact far more serious than that, as the doctors found that a blood clot had formed within her skull that could have killed or disabled her. She had previously developed a blood clot in her leg some years before as a result of her non-stop flying around the US during the 1998 mid-term election campaign. She was now back on blood-thinners again, and no more flying as Secretary of State. It took six months for her to recover fully from her concussion.

As the assessments started to be written of her role as

Secretary of State, even her admirers had to acknowl-edge that there had been few spectacular achievements, with Michael Kinsley of Bloomberg observing ungal-lantly that the still convalescing Hillary 'looked terrible', and that she had worked herself to death, with limited accomplishments. Obama and Hillary appeared together in a farewell performance for her on *60 Minutes*. Hillary told the BBC reporter Kim Ghattas, who had travelled around the world with her, 'I won't lie to you, I'm tired.'[81]

Two weeks after his 6 November victory in the elec-tion, Obama asked Hillary if she might stay on for another year, as Leon Panetta also was intending to resign as Defense Secretary. Hillary declined and Obama did not persist.

Hillary's response to criticism of a lack of spectacular achievement as Secretary of State was that diplomacy is a relay race in which every senior figure must do what they can, when they can. They can play only with the cards that are dealt them, must seek to exploit what opportunities they can and try to pass on to their suc-cessors the chance to build on what they had sought to achieve. The only one of her recent predecessors who could claim to have achieved more than her was James Baker, who had all of Hillary's qualities and then some, and a much more favourable international environment in which to operate.

Hillary's faith in public diplomacy led her to exaggerate at times the possible impact of US declarations of intent. She waxed lyrical about Obama's 2009 speech at Cairo University seeking to 're-calibrate' the US relationship with the Muslim world and at his declaration at the summit of the Americas, also in 2009, about an 'equal partnership' with Latin America, which was unlikely of itself to persuade most Latin Americans to see it that way. Her memoir skates around the fact that most of America's traditional allies in the Middle East felt that they could place more confidence in George W. Bush than the semi-detached Barack Obama, a sentiment prevalent also in eastern Europe.

It remains easy to make fun of Hillary's earnestness. No other Secretary of State is likely to launch a 'Global Clean Cookstove Initiative', together with a score of other 'global initiatives'.

But no one could complain that Hillary was semi-detached. She believed in trying to establish personal relationships on a world-wide scale and in listening to America's allies even if at times they drove her to distraction. In the process she earned the respect of the huge US press contingent that accompanied her around the globe, and of the international press as well, completing the transformation of what had started as her edgy and quite often adversarial relationship with the media. The

Hillary they found themselves travelling with was a lot more likeable, more fun and much more comfortable in her skin than the unelected partner of Bill Clinton in the White House had been. Returning on her plane from a trip abroad, Hillary, her team and the accompanying press found themselves watching a film in which one of the characters declared: 'Never trust a woman in a pant suit … The world can't afford any more Hillary Clintons!' Hillary and co. all fell about laughing.[82]

Above all, she succeeded in passing the Rudyard Kipling test of winning the respect of her peers. The immensely experienced Bob Gates, who had served in several administrations, Republican and Democrat, culminating as CIA director, then Secretary for Defense, could not stand some members of the White House foreign policy team. But he had nothing but praise for Hillary as a dependable partner and determined defender of US interests. She got on just as well with the almost equally experienced Leon Panetta, former White House chief of staff, then Obama's CIA director and Gates's successor as Secretary for Defense.

In 2011 Hillary had clashed with Panetta, then head of the CIA, by supporting the US ambassador's request that he should be forewarned of drone strikes in Pakistan, which Panetta flatly rejected. In 2012 Panetta wanted to issue a draconian warning to Iran for firing at a US drone, which Hillary opposed. Hillary told Panetta: 'This is really nice to be yelling at you again. Last time you were on the line (in a video conference) and it was just not as fun as yelling at you face to face.'[83]

Shortly after Obama's re-election, General Petraeus resigned as CIA director over an affair with his biographer. Hillary, who really admired Petraeus, as he did her, went out of her way to express her sympathy. 'I have a little experience,' she observed.

General Petraeus returned the kindness by declaring that she would be a 'tremendous' President. He would be certain to be offered a senior post in a future Clinton administration, if there is one.

The same is true for her counterparts around the world. It is difficult to find any of them prepared to say anything negative about Hillary, and not just because they might find themselves dealing with her again as President. The most they will say, which she would regard as a compliment, is that she is very American. Apart from regarding the United States as 'the indispensable nation' and what Abraham Lincoln described as the 'last best hope' of humanity in dealing with major crises around the world, she also believes, however, that other countries would be better off if they were more like America, an opinion not shared by a good many of them and certainly not by the Chinese.

Helmut Schmidt used to complain, with reference particularly to Jimmy Carter, about the unfortunate need for on-the-job training of US Presidents in foreign policy. No one is going to be able to make that allegation about Hillary. The key partners who have dealt with her, and those who know her, are unanimous in believing that Hillary, if elected, would continue to seek from the White House to pursue a more active and less passive approach to foreign policy, in which she has a far more passionate interest than Obama. With a darkening scene in the Middle East and a crisis with Russia over Ukraine, a good many of America's friends and allies probably do feel that the world is ready for Hillary. Can the same be said of the United States?

CHAPTER 23

'SUPERPOWERS DON'T GET TO RETIRE'

AMERICAN CRITICS, DEMOCRAT and Republican, of Obama's diplomacy have depicted it as a US version of European foreign policy consisting, as they see it, of statements that much of what is happening in the world is 'unacceptable' or 'deplorable', without actually intending to do much about it, as in Syria. Hillary's successor as Secretary of State, John Kerry, did want to take action in response to the Syrian use of chemical weapons, has denounced his

Russian counterpart Lavrov's 'Kafkaesque' lying about the Russian interventions in Ukraine and has tried hard to broker an agreement between the two main competing candidates in the Afghan elections. He also has led the negotiations about the Iranian nuclear programme, a problem that is a long way from being resolved. He has been trying just as hard as Hillary.

So far as the White House is concerned, however, the perception has remained that the President is not very interested in foreign policy, nor very involved, and that he is highly resistant to any further entanglements abroad. The Obama doctrine, as set out in his May 2014 speech to the US military academy at West Point, made clear his desire to replace US military involvement with diplomacy and economic statecraft wherever possible. The US, he argues, has a 'hard-earned humility' about its ability to determine events in other countries.

This more detached view stems from the character and temperament of the President. The Obama White House takes comfort from, and has been influenced by, polling showing that the public reaction to protracted and unpopular wars in Iraq and Afghanistan has been to question why the US should constantly have to take the lead in grappling with overseas crises, particularly with its allies unlikely to do more themselves, leading to a conclusion that other countries in general should be left to get on as best they can. Hillary regards this as demonstrating a lack of leadership. For the Republicans, Rand Paul, echoing his 'America first' predecessor, Senator Robert Taft, is opposed to the US acting as a 'knight errant' in other parts of the world.

For Obama's critics, the passive and more detached attitude of the White House has caused great concern among America's allies in eastern Europe, Asia and the Middle East and has encouraged dangerous adventurism by Putin in Ukraine and aggressive behaviour by China in the South China Sea. The French Foreign Minister, Laurent Fabius, has observed that the United States 'gives the impression of no longer wanting to be drawn into crises' and that, as nobody can replace the Americans from a military point of view, they may simply be allowed to fester. The Republican senator Bob Corker of the Senate foreign relations committee reports allies constantly questioning him as to whether, if some crisis worsens, 'the US will be there'.

Robert Kagan describes this phenomenon as the US having become 'world weary', creating the risk of a more unstable and dangerous international environment in which rogue states and aggressive rulers would be able to operate relatively unchecked.[84] Asked about Obama's foreign policy mantra 'Don't do stupid stuff', Hillary described this as not an organising principle worthy of a great nation, bringing instant retaliation from Obama supporters. She takes, she says, a more old-fashioned and optimistic view of what the US can achieve and promised to 'hug out' her differences with the President in the course of their respective holiday stays on Martha's Vineyard.

Kagan's influential essay on this subject in *New Republic*, also in May 2014, is entitled: 'Superpowers Don't Get to Retire', a sentiment with which she would wholeheartedly agree. As the Republican contenders other than Rand Paul attack the perceived passivity of Obama foreign policy, she will position herself as the advocate of the 'indispensable nation' on which America's allies continue to depend and without which most international crises have little chance of being contained, let alone resolved.[85]

Henry Kissinger has long been a critic of the Woodrow Wilsonian 'idealistic' strand in American foreign policy* and the belief that western-style democracy should be exported to areas of the world where it has never been known to flourish before, which he describes as a Sisyphean task. In his latest book, *World Order*, however, he argues that the United States in

---

* When Wilson produced his Fourteen Points for the better ordering of the universe following World War I, the French Prime Minister Georges Clemenceau protested: 'But the Lord God had only ten!'

its own interests cannot abandon its essential leadership role in dealing with overseas crises. The actions of the Islamic State jihadists require an immediate and forceful response. The US must contain Iranian nuclear ambitions and those of Putin in Ukraine. He has publicly deplored the passivity of the Obama administration and the alienation of America's traditional allies in the Middle East.[86]

Reviewing his book in the *Washington Post*, Hillary declared her agreement with most of it, confirming the worst suspicions of her left-wing critics by describing Kissinger as a friend and someone she consulted as Secretary of State. No other nation, in her view, 'can bring together the necessary coalitions and provide the necessary capabilities to meet today's global threats'.[87] Kissinger is an admirer of Hillary, despite her 'Wilsonian' tendencies, saying that as a Republican he would have a conflict, but in effect endorsing her as someone who could be counted on to uphold America's role in the world ('She would be a good President').

Hillary has learned the lessons of Iraq and Afghanistan. She has no intention of getting the US involved in further land wars in Asia or the Middle East and will be very cautious indeed about American 'boots on the ground'. There would be no return to what she regards as the militarism of George W. Bush and Cheney. But nor would she be as hesitant about the targeted use of force in cases like Syria and the activities of the Islamic State and other declared enemies of the US. She will be determined to reassure the allies that the US will indeed be there but, in relation for instance to Ukraine, she will want to know whether the Europeans will show backbone in responding to Russian aggression, reducing their dependence on Russian energy supplies, and to what extent they are actually prepared to contribute to their own defence. Allies looking forward to a return of Hillary, as quite a few of them are, will need to work out the answers to these questions, which will be asked by any future US President.

*   *   *

As for the United Kingdom, Hillary has a lot of British friends or acquaintances. She admires the country, the people and its history and values the especially close relationship with the United States. On most international issues, she has found her British counterparts to be among her closest allies. She will continue to pay tribute to a special relationship ('Special in my mind'), as she did as Secretary of State.[88]

This does not mean that the UK should expect any special favours from her. Britain will be valued and have influence according to its contribution. She shares the general American dismay at the further cuts in our armed forces, affecting in Bob Gates's view, Britain's ability to act in future as a fully effective military ally of the United States. The British armed forces, now reduced to a single tank regiment, cannot give the US the support they have delivered in the past, though because of shared intelligence and close military ties they are more capable than others of operating with their US counterparts. Their contribution in Afghanistan was valued highly by Hillary and British support will remain important to America in dealing with problems like those posed by the Islamic State, though no one in the US can understand how the UK can believe that the threat can be contained by dealing with it only in Iraq. The US also will continue to rely on the French military in dealing with the Islamic insurgents in north and west Africa. Hillary's view on the realities of power, however, was clearly expressed in July 2014 when she described Angela Merkel as 'Europe's greatest leader', though Germany remains unable to give the US effective military support.

Hillary was shocked by the vote of the House of Commons against action in response to the use of chemical weapons by the Syrian regime. She could scarcely believe this reaction to the killing of 1,400 civilians. For this and other reasons, there is unlikely to be any meeting of minds with Ed Miliband. She does not agree with him about Hamas and Gaza. He sounds to her like old Labour. She had hoped that Gordon Brown would be succeeded by David Miliband.

Hillary would be dismayed if Britain left the European Union, not because she does not agree with many British criticisms of the functioning of the EU (as a matter of fact, she does agree with most of them) but because, from the US point of view, she would fear that a British exit would result in a more inward-looking, protectionist and hyper-bureaucratic entity, with American influence and the ability to pursue jointly worthwhile initiatives, such as the Transatlantic Trade and Investment Partnership, diminished within it. The value of US investments in Britain would be affected unless there were continuing guaranteed trade access to the EU.

She would, however, be very cautious about getting involved in a UK political controversy. She is well aware of the view of most US economists that the European Union has become an over-regulated, high cost and low growth economic area, an example to be avoided by the United States. She can understand the lack of desire of the British to be governed increasingly from Brussels. She would subscribe to the proposition that Britain should remain a member of a reformed EU (assuming that is achievable). If re-negotiation became a real prospect after the British election, she would urge Angela Merkel and Donald Tusk as President of the European Council to seek to reach an accommodation with Britain.

In office, she would continue to try to do business primarily with the leaders of Germany, Britain and France, with whom she feels a lot more familiar than in dealing with the Brussels institutions. If there were to be a British exit, which she would do what she could to avoid, she would want to see the closest possible continuing economic and political relationship between Britain and the United States.

As for Scottish independence, Americans were surprised that the United Kingdom should be prepared to allow one of its component parts to vote on whether to secede. Friends of the United Kingdom in the US, of whom Hillary is one, were relieved at the outcome, as a vote for separation would have been seen as a 'diminution of Britain' and a massive distraction for a key ally at a time when its support is needed in dealing with major international challenges.

CHAPTER 24

READY FOR HILLARY?

T HE MORE CHALLENGING question is
whether the United States, even today, is ready
for Hillary Clinton. As of now, she clearly has
a better chance than anyone else of being the next President of the US. Hillary has everything in place for her
second run at the Presidency. The decision for her is not
whether to run, but whether to stop running.

For nearly all the necessary infrastructure already is in
place for her campaign. From the time she stood down
as Secretary of State, a 'super PAC' (political action

committee), Ready for Hillary, has been in place to raise
funds for her. Such super PACs, at arm's length from the
candidate, have no constraints on the amount of money
they can raise, though Ready for Hillary has an individual subscription limit of $25,000. One of the patrons
of Ready for Hillary is George Soros. Another Hillary-
related organisation, Correct the Record, is ready to deal
instantly with negative information about her. Last time,
she was concerned not to run as a female candidate. This
time, there would be a more straightforward appeal to
women and attack on the glass ceiling, with another
organisation, Emily's List, intended to rally the sister-
hood behind Madam President. Another super PAC,
Priorities USA, a key fund-raiser for Obama and led
by his former deputy chief of staff, Jim Messina, also
has been aligning itself with Hillary.

Hillary's account of her time as Secretary of State,
Hard Choices, has sold over a million copies, but has
been given a hard time by the US press because it so
obviously has been written in terms designed to avoid
any hostages to fortune in relation to a future challenge
for the Presidency. It is in fact very informative about
US foreign policy, but devoid of the sort of detail about
administration infighting provided by her counterpart,
Bob Gates, in his more no-holds-barred memoir, *Duty*.

Meanwhile, in the mid-term election campaign,

Democratic Party candidates have been showing little interest in having a President with low approval ratings campaign for them. The person most in demand to support them in their constituencies is Bill Clinton. Few who know Hillary really believe that she can be stopped from declaring her candidature after the New Year by anything other than a medical opinion, backed by concern from Chelsea about her mother's health. Her brand new status as a grandmother is not going to stop her, provided she can withstand the campaign.

But two years is a long time in politics, particularly for a 67-year-old faced with eighteen months of non-stop electioneering. Ronald Reagan took this in his stride at the same age, but he knew how to pace himself. He spent far less time than Hillary imposing stress on himself (and more in the gym). Asked if America is ready for a 69-year-old female President, Hillary described the question as a joke. 'We've had so many grandfathers in the White House' that to rule out a grandmother would be ridiculous.

With the American public, Hillary's approval ratings have hit two peaks. The first was during the Monica Lewinsky affair, when two out of three Americans accorded her a sympathy vote, considering that she was conducting herself with dignity in extremely difficult personal circumstances. The second surge, much longer in duration, came in terms of roughly the same

level of approval for her performance as Secretary of
State, a post in which the incumbent is expected to act as
a non-partisan figure. In her term as Secretary, Hillary
was not able to attend the Democratic Party convention.

As Hillary's approval rating reached 66 per cent, she was
well aware that these numbers would drop back dramatically the minute she re-engaged in party politics and, sure
enough, her ratings soon fell back to around 50 per cent.

Within her own party, the left wing were and are distrustful of her, particularly on national security issues.
The current standard-bearer of the left, scourge of Wall
Street and Obama favourite, Senator Elizabeth Warren
of Massachusetts, is no fan of Hillary, who she regards
as elitist, out of touch and much too cosy with the
investment banks that helped to precipitate the economic meltdown and a closet Republican in foreign
policy. Her current mantra that 'I am not running for
President' is designed to keep open the option of doing
so. It remains to be seen if she will risk running against
Hillary, but it is not the desire that would be lacking.
She would pose a serious challenge on the left of the
party and cause problems for Hillary in New England,
but may struggle to compete nation-wide.

The Vice-President, Joe Biden, with whom Hillary
got on well, despite their policy differences (at the end
of each phone call he would say 'I love you, darling!'),

has said that he can see no reason why he should not run. But he would be seventy-four in 2016 and his poll numbers are nowhere near Hillary's. In an earlier bid for the Presidency, he ran into trouble by plagiarising a speech from, of all people, Neil Kinnock.

Among the party's rising stars, Andrew Cuomo, Governor of New York, would not be likely to run against Hillary. There is no sign on the Democratic political horizon of a new cult figure, another Barack Obama, capable of mounting a potentially devastating challenge to her. Once again, the press will not want a coronation. But given her massive advantage in fund-raising and track record, that is what they might get, leaving Hillary, potentially, with an important advantage vis-à-vis a fractious and squabbling Republican Party with, at present, a plethora of candidates seeking to oppose her.

A decision by Hillary not to run would leave the Democratic Party in disarray, reducing their chances of retaining the Presidency and leading to a free-for-all involving some or all of Joe Biden, Andrew Cuomo, Elizabeth Warren, Rahm Emmanuel, Mayor of Chicago, and Kirsten Gillibrand, Hillary's impressive successor as senator for New York, plus others too. While a convincing candidate could emerge from this field, he or she would not have anything like the national stature Hillary has acquired.

In 2008 Barack Obama, running against her, was successful in depicting Hillary as a highly divisive figure,
incapable of overcoming partisanship in Washington
and unifying the country in the manner he aimed to do.
This was a remarkable feat, given that he had the most
'liberal', i.e. left-wing, voting record of any senator. But
many believed it at the time.

They have ceased to believe it of Obama as President.
Hillary is a dyed-in-the-wool Democrat, left of centre
on most social issues. But in the Senate and as Secretary of State, she showed herself ready to work with
the moderate wing of the Republican Party and, like
her husband, would try to do so in the White House,
if she got there.

The Republican leaderships in the House and the Senate, meanwhile, have been trying to re-assert themselves
vis-à-vis the Tea Party and other right-wing ideologues,
who have turned out to be good at winning primaries
among the party faithful, but have very limited appeal
to the electorate at large.

Nevertheless, in an important sense, the election
ought to be the Republicans, to lose. The tide clearly
has been running their way, as evidenced again in the
mid-term elections. They will be arguing that, except
in foreign policy, Hillary would simply represent an
Obama third term. The Obama Presidency appears to

have run almost completely out of steam, with the President anxious to get away from Washington, appearing at times semi-detached, and the Republicans making further gains in Congress. The situation would seem to be ripe for a populist, down-to-earth, grass-roots Republican contender able to talk to ordinary Americans in language they can understand. This would potentially be the best antidote to Hillary as well.

The person cast for this role by much of the Republican establishment was the popular, successful, heavyweight (in fact seriously overweight) Governor of New Jersey, Chris Christie. A formidable campaigner, he would be seeking to portray himself as more in touch with middle America than her. But he has been damaged by the transport authority scandal in New Jersey, with the Governor's aides restricting access for several days to the George Washington Bridge into New York for residents of the adjoining Fort Lee district, whose Democratic Mayor had fallen out with the Governor.

The self-styled libertarian, critic of the National Security Agency's monitoring activities and opponent of drone strikes, Senator Rand Paul of Kentucky is regarded by the internationalist wing of the party as a downright isolationist. Other potential contenders, such as the right-wing senator Ted Cruz from Texas and Senator Marco Rubio of Florida, have important sections

of the party opposed to them. The Republican nomination will not be settled without a potentially damaging
fight between the right and left wings of the party. The
Tea Party representatives are in the habit of describing
their more moderate colleagues as 'rhinos' (Republicans
in name only). They in turn are described by the party
leadership, not only in private, as 'the Taliban'.

The demographics favour Hillary. In most recent elections, the Republicans have had a clear majority among
white males. But there are not enough of them for that to
come anywhere close to delivering victory. Hillary can
expect to have a commanding lead among black Americans and hopes to have one also in the rapidly growing
Hispanic electorate, though that could depend on the
Republican candidate. Among women, the Republicans
still are handicapped by a position in principle (though
hardly in practice) against abortion that offends a huge
swathe of women voters who think that such a decision
should be left to them.

Does all this mean that Hillary should be a shoo-
in for President? Absolutely not. She would be under
relentless scrutiny, particularly as regards her health.
A fainting fit or two under the pressure of the campaign could fatally undermine her. She will be targeted
mercilessly. Asked recently if she did not fear further
invasions of her privacy, she replied cheerfully: 'What

privacy is there left?' Rupert Murdoch has said patron-
isingly that he could 'live with' Hillary as President. But
that will not prevent the Fox TV channels and the other
right-wing commentators attacking her every inch of
the way. She will find particularly hurtful the allegations about Benghazi, as Christopher Stevens was her
personal choice as ambassador to Libya and it was to
her that it fell to try to console his family.

Hillary has not got this far without a clear understanding that US politics is a contact sport and one in which
no holds are barred. She already is experiencing another
slew of re-hashed stories about her husband's private life.
George W. Bush's key political advisor, Karl Rove, made
the extraordinary suggestion that Hillary may have suffered brain damage as a result of her concussion! She has
said that her full medical records will be released if she
declares her candidacy. In response to gratuitous attacks,
she will need to curb her natural tendency to react aggressively under fire, at the risk of sounding shrill rather than
the statesmanlike frontrunner.

Another factor she will have to manage is that of
Hillaryland. This fiercely loyal, highly professional,
competent and dynamic group of women around her
has just one problem: they are all too much like her.
They are believers in all the politically correct causes on
the east and west coasts, but a distance removed from

the preoccupations of the 'fly over' states in between. Whoever is brought in to help correct that balance will not find it easy, given their proximity to her.

She also has to work out how far to distance herself from Barack Obama, which she has started to do on foreign policy. Hitherto she has been careful not to allow the press a field day with stories of real or supposed differences with the President. When he delivered his greatest domestic achievement, the extension of healthcare insurance to millions who did not have it, Hillary was thrilled at the accomplishment of what had been her own cause. The roll out of the scheme has been fraught with difficulty and many features of it remain unpopular, but Hillary would be the last to permit any turning back.

In running to succeed him, however, she will have to illustrate in what respects she would be different to a President whose approval ratings are historically very low, and this is going to put a strain on the relationship between them. Whatever his personal feelings about her are (and with Obama, you never really know), that will not stop some members of his team taking shots at her, questioning whether she can really connect with ordinary Americans. Hillary, for her part, stated recently that voters should ask themselves two questions about any candidate for President. Firstly, did they have a vision for the country? Secondly, how effective would they be in actually getting things done to realise that vision, a reflection seen as implied criticism of Obama. So long as Joe Biden is in the race, Obama anyway may decline to choose between them, but Hillary will have to show that she would be different, without too badly burning her bridges with the White House, a feat that already is proving quite difficult to perform.

The US budget deficit has declined dramatically. But Hillary knows that the most intractable long-term economic problem the country faces will be the budgetary consequences of the entitlement programmes, especially Medicare and Medicaid, which most of her constituency believe should be defended at all costs. Obama has sought to park the problem, by refusing to limit entitlements until the Republicans agree to some increase in taxes, and this shadow theatre will continue for some time. Hillary will seek to parlay some future limits on entitlements against tax reform, eliminating many of the myriad tax exemptions which are a feature of the current US system. Obama has tried this, but she would be likely to attempt to do so with more conviction and engagement with Congress.

In dealing (or failing to deal) with this problem, one threat will not impress her. Hillary has seen the Republicans in Congress on two occasions, first against her husband, then against Obama, forcing a partial government shut-down in their efforts to impose spending cuts on the administration. On both occasions, this tactic has back-fired, proving unpopular and unsustainable. As Hillary has pointed out, with acerbity, it amounted to refusal to fund expenditure on programmes already voted for by Congress, causing the Chinese, with their huge investments in US Treasury bills, and America's allies to ask what on earth was going on in Washington. Campaigning for her friend and Clinton fund-raiser Terry McAuliffe's election as Governor of Virginia, Hillary accused the Republicans of resorting to scorched-earth tactics.

Hillary will, however, be vulnerable to Republican charges that, while very close to Wall Street (anathema on Main Street), she has never shown much interest in, empathy for or understanding of the US business community at large. While mainly business audiences have been paying huge fees for appearances from her, the relationship with the Obama administration has been fraught for the past six years and many of them are not convinced that she would be much better. The 'economic' conferences and seminars she has been organising are all about the social issues with which she is preoccupied, displaying relatively little interest in how wealth and jobs actually are created and what practical measures might help to get the US economy moving again. Hillary does not see any irony in appearing at a Goldman Sachs event for a reputed $200,000, then following this with a speech at Yale about inequality.

A Hillary candidacy has conjured up the possibility of a dynastic battle in 2016 with George W. Bush's elder brother, Jeb. A very successful two-term Governor of Florida with stellar reform credentials, especially in education, well out on the left of his party on several issues, for which he will be attacked in the Republican primaries, Jeb Bush is a strong advocate of immigration reform. That would entail legalising a lot of at present illegal immigrants. Speaking fluent Spanish and with a wife from Mexico, he won a majority of the Hispanic votes in Florida and the Republicans will badly need to attract more Hispanic support if they are to regain the White House.

If Jeb Bush could overcome right-wing resistance to win the Republican nomination, Americans would find themselves witnessing the curious spectacle of two multi-millionaires talking eloquently about inequality and the plight of the supposedly forgotten American middle class who, though living longer, have found that they are not getting richer any more. The odds are that Bush would know at least as well how to improve things for them as Hillary, but he may not get the chance to show it. The US economy at last is showing signs

of recovering much more strongly than those in con-
tinental Europe and that recovery, if sustained, should
help her in an election in which economics will not be
her strongest suit.

*   *   *

The prospects for a Hillary candidacy can be analysed to
death. Beyond the Democratic nomination, the demographics and the reputation she has established since her
election to the Senate and tenure as Secretary of State
should make her favourite to win the general election
as well. Favourites do not always win, as she learned
the hard way in 2008. But an older, wiser Hillary, just
as ambitious, but more likeable and less tense, is better
equipped to win the prize today than she was before, to
a point at which it may well be that she could only be
beaten by herself, by doubts about her health and ability to withstand a two-year campaign, or reversion to
a younger, shriller and more partisan version of herself.
To her critics, there is little to suggest that she would
make a great President. But, even they would have to
concede that she would be likely to prove a thoroughly
competent one.

BIBLIOGRAPHY

THE PROBLEM IN writing about Hillary Rodham Clinton is the superabundance of sources.
She has been the subject of saturation coverage
by the media for the past twenty-two years, in particular in the *New York Times*, *Washington Post* and *Wall
Street Journal*. The coverage is equally comprehensive and constantly updated on all the Clinton-related
websites.

The most valuable sources of all are her two auto-
biographical works, *Living History* and *Hard Choices*,
published by Simon & Schuster, New York, respectively
in 2001 and 2014. Some of the papers relating to her
time as First Lady have been released by the William J.

Clinton Presidential Library in Little Rock. The papers
of her friend Diane Blair are held at the University of
Arkansas in Fayetteville. Bill Clinton's own memoir,
My Life, was published by Vintage Books, New York,
in 2004.

Among the numerous biographies of her, friendly
and hostile, the best-known are Gail Sheehy's account
of Hillary's life and career up to and including her time
as First Lady, *Hillary's Choice*, published by Ballan-
tine Books, New York, in 2000, and Carl Bernstein's
A Woman in Charge, published by Random House,
New York, in 2007.

The best accounts of her contest with Barack Obama
in 2008 for the Democratic Party candidacy for the Presidency are to be found in *Game Change: Obama and
the Clintons, McCain and Palin, and the Race of a Lifetime* by John Heilemann and Mark Halperin, published
by Harper Collins, New York, in 2010, and in Dan Balz
and Haynes Johnson's *The Battle for America 2008*,
Viking Books, New York, 2009. Bob Woodward's *Obama's Wars*, published by Simon & Schuster, New York,
in 2010, is relevant to her time as Secretary of State. A
detailed account of her activities as Secretary, based on
briefing by Hillaryland, is to be found in Jonathan Allen
and Amie Parnes's *HRC: State Secrets and the Rebirth
of Hillary Clinton*, Crown Publishers, New York, 2014.

Apart from her own account in *Hard Choices*, however, the best source material on her role as Secretary of State is to be found in Robert Gates's memoir, *Duty*, published by Alfred A. Knopf, New York, in 2014 and in that of Leon Panetta, *Worthy Fights*, published by Penguin in New York, also in 2014.

References to a number of the more important press articles about her are to be found in the text.

Other relevant books about her, friendly or hostile, include:

Bedell Smith, Sally, *For Love of Politics: Inside the Clinton White House* (Random House: New York, 2007).

Brock, David, *The Seduction of Hillary Rodham* (The Free Press; New York, 1996).

Gerth, Jeff and Van Natta, Don, *Her Way: the Hopes and Ambitions of Hillary Rodham Clinton* (Little Brown; New York, 1996).

Ghattas, Kim, *The Secretary: a Journey with Hillary Clinton from Beirut to the Heart of American Power* (Times Books; New York, 2013).

Maraniss, David, *First in His Class: a Biography of Bill Clinton* (Simon & Schuster; New York, 1995).

Morris, Roger, *Partners in Power: the Clintons and Their America* (Henry Holt; New York, 1996).

Olson, Barbara, *Hell to Pay: the Unfolding Story of Hillary Rodham Clinton* (Regnery Publishing; Washington, 1999).

Troy, Gil, *Hillary Rodham Clinton: Polarizing First Lady* (Kansas University Press; Lawrence, 2006).

ACKNOWLEDGEMENTS

I AM VERY GRATEFUL to Iain Dale, James Stephens and Victoria Godden for their invaluable help and support in producing this book, to Herbert Ragan at the William J. Clinton Presidential Library and Pete Souza at the White House, to the Library staff at the House of Lords, to Katie Gareh, Doug Cooper and Caroline Cook for their help with the manuscript, and to Marie-France Renwick for her assistance with the illustrations.

Several friends of Hillary and a long-standing member of Hillaryland have kindly helped to verify some of the episodes described in the book. The opinions expressed in it, they have asked me to make clear, are my own.

ENDNOTES

1 Hillary to the author and others at the time

2 Hillary Rodham Clinton, *Hard Choices*, pp. 180–7

3 Ibid., pp. 191–6. Robert Gates, *Duty*, pp. 538–46. Leon Panetta, *Worthy Fights*, pp. 306–31

4 Hillary Rodham Clinton, *Living History*, p. 1

5 Ibid., p. 33. Carl Bernstein, *A Woman in Charge*, p. 53

6 HRC, *Living History*, p. 38

7 *Life* magazine, 20 June 1969

8 Gail Sheehy, *Hillary's Choice*, p. 73

9 HRC, *Living History*, pp. 52, 54

10 Peter Sussman ed., *Decca, The Letters of Jessica Mitford* (Weiden-feld & Nicolson, 2004), pp. 527–9, 661

11   Hillary Clinton, 'Children under the Law', *Harvard Educational Review*, 1973, Vol. 43 (4), pp. 487–514

12   HRC, *Living History,* p. 83. Bernstein op. cit., pp. 132–4

13   HRC, *Living History,* p. 97

14   *American Spectator*, August 1991

15   HRC, *Living History,* p. 133

16   *New York Times* magazine, 23 May 1993

17   HRC, *Living History,* p. 178

18   Bill Bradley quoted in Bernstein, op. cit., p. 304

19   HRC, *Living History,* p. 235

20   Lisa Caputo note, August 1995, in the First Lady papers released by the William J Clinton Presidential Library

21   HRC, *Living History,* pp. 305–6. *New York Times,* 6 September 1995

22   HRC, *Living History,* pp. 422–4

23   Ibid., pp. 440–6

24   Ibid., p. 450

25   Ibid., pp. 465–73

26   Ibid., p. 501

27   John Heilemann and Mark Halperin, *Game Change: Obama and the Clintons, McCain and Palin and the Race of a Lifetime*, pp. 7–8

28   *New York Times*, 21 February 2007.

29   Heilemann and Halperin, op. cit., pp. 239–240

30   HRC, *Hard Choices,* pp. 1–4, 12–19

31   Joseph S. Nye, *Soft Power: The Means to Success in World Politics* (Public Affairs; New York, 2004), p. xiii

32 *New York Times*, 10 January 2009

33 Allen and Parnes, *HRC*, p. 85

34 Gates, op. cit., pp. 283–290

35 Hillary Clinton, 'America's Pacific Century', *Foreign Policy*, October 2011

36 HRC, *Hard Choices,* p. 63

37 HRC, *Hard Choices,* p. 79. Gates, op. cit., pp. 414–9

38 HRC, *Hard Choices,* pp. 101, 118–25. Kim Ghattas, *The Secretary*, pp 301–4

39 HRC, *Hard Choices,* p. 232. Allen and Parnes, op. cit., pp. 136–8

40 Allen and Parnes, op. cit., pp. 194–8. Gates, op. cit., p. 407

41 Gates, op. cit., pp. 329, 404–10. HRC, *Hard Choices,* p. 239

42 HRC, *Hard Choices,* pp. 234–5

43 On Hillary and WikiLeaks, see Kim Ghattas, op. cit., pp. 195–209

44 Gates, op. cit., pp. 288, 336–7, 375–6. HRC, *Hard Choices,* pp. 129–34

45 Gates, op. cit., pp. 377–85. HRC, *Hard Choices,* p. 148. Panetta, op. cit., pp. 254–5. See also Bob Woodward, *Obama's Wars*

46 HRC, *Hard Choices,* pp. 152–3

47 Gates, op. cit., pp. 481–2

48 Ibid., pp. 483–502

49 HRC, *Hard Choices,* pp. 159–62

50 Gates, op. cit., pp. 564–5, 585

51 Statement by Secretary Clinton, US Department of State, 3 July 2012

52 Gates, op. cit., pp. 584–7

53 HRC, *Hard Choices,* pp. 134–7. Allen and Parnes, op. cit., pp. 71–2

54 HRC, *Hard Choices,* p. 137

55 Ibid., pp. 303, 316–26

56 Ibid., pp. 478–87. Allen and Parnes, op. cit., pp 329–33

57 Gates, op. cit., pp. 504–10

58 HRC, *Hard Choices,* p. 344

59 Ibid., p. 377

60 Ibid., pp. 356–60. Allen and Parnes, op. cit., pp. 207–12

61 HRC, *Hard Choices,* pp. 462–9. Gates, op. cit., pp. 523, 591

62 *New York Times,* 2 February 2013. Panetta, op. cit., p. 450

63 HRC, *Hard Choices,* p. 420

64 Ibid., pp. 421–5, 439–41. Allen and Parnes, op. cit., pp. 186–91, 324–5

65 HRC, *Hard Choices,* p. 496

66 Allen and Parnes, op. cit., pp. 171–81. Ibid., pp. 492–505

67 HRC, *Hard Choices,* pp. 207–11, 224–5

68 Gates, op. cit., pp. 511–13. Ibid., pp. 366–7

69 HRC, *Hard Choices,* pp. 368–9. Allen and Parnes, op. cit., pp. 213–20

70 HRC, *Hard Choices,* p. 372. Allen and Parnes, op. cit., pp. 221–2

71 Gates, op. cit., pp. 517–22

72 CNN, 18 October 2011

73 US Senate Select Committee on Intelligence: Review of the Terrorist Attacks on US facilities in Benghazi, Libya, September 11–12, 2012, published on 15 January 2014

74   Remarks by Secretary Clinton, US Department of State, 2 September 2012

75   Accountability Review Board Report, 19 December 2012, http://1.usa.gov/TYkdAW. Allen and Parnes, op. cit., pp. 298–309.

76   HRC, *Hard Choices*, pp. 411–14

77   HRC, *Living History*, pp. 402–3

78   HRC, *Hard Choices*, pp. 295–7

79   Ibid., pp. 271–2

80   Ibid., pp. 280–1. Allen and Parnes, op. cit., pp. 166–9

81   Hillary Clinton interview with Kim Ghattas, BBC, 14 June 2011

82   HRC, *Hard Choices*, p. 41

83   Ibid., p. 184

84   Robert Kagan, 'Superpowers Don't Get to Retire', *New Republic*, 26 May 2014

85   Henry Kissinger, *World Order: Reflections on the Character of Nations and the Course of History*, Allen Lane, 2014

86   *Sunday Times*, 7 September 2014

87   Hillary Clinton review of *World Order*, *Washington Post*, 4 September 2014. Kissinger on Hillary ('She would be a good President'), *Washington Post*, 7 September 2014

88   HRC, *Living History*, p. 450, *Hard Choices*, p. 207

INDEX